Editor
Heather Douglas

Illustrator
Clint McKnight

Cover Artist
Brenda Di Antonis

Managing Editor
Ina Massler Levin, M.A.

Creative Director
Karen J. Goldfluss, M.S. Ed.

Art Production Manager
Kevin Barnes

Art Coordinator
Renée Christine Yates

Imaging
Rosa C. See
Len Swierski
Nathan Rivera

Publisher

Mary D. Smith, M.S. Ed.

101 LESSONS
Vocabulary Words In Context

Grades 3-5

The water was becoming very turbulent.

A baby swan is called a cygnet.

Includes
Over 500 Words
in a Variety of Contexts
• Nonfiction Articles
• E-mail
• Fliers
• Advertisements
• Recipes
• Stories

Includes
Standards &
Benchmarks

Authors

Greg Camden, M.A.
and
Eric Migliaccio

Teacher Created Resources, Inc.
6421 Industry Way
Westminster, CA 92683
www.teachercreated.com

ISBN-13: 978-1-4206-8142-0

© 2007 Teacher Created Resources, Inc.

Made in U.S.A.

Teacher Created Resources

Table of Contents

Table of Contents *(cont.)*

Standards

101 Lessons: Vocabulary Words in Context meets the following language-arts standards and benchmarks for the Grades 3–5 classroom. (Used with permission from McREL. Copyright 2004 McREL. Mid-continent Research for Education and Learning. 2550 S. Parker Road, Suite 500, Aurora, CO 80014. Telephone: (303) 337-0990. Website: www.mcrel.org/standards-benchmarks.)

> **Standard 5: Uses the general skills and strategies of the reading process**

- Uses phonetic and structural analysis techniques, syntactic structure, and semantic context to decode unknown words (e.g., vowel patterns, complex word families, syllabication, root words, affixes)

- Use a variety of context clues to decode unknown words (e.g., draws on earlier reading, read ahead)

- Use word reference materials (e.g., glossary, dictionary, thesaurus) to determine the meaning, pronunciation, and derivations of unknown words

- Understands level-appropriate reading vocabulary (e.g., synonyms, antonyms, homophones, multi-meaning words)

Introduction

There are many vocabulary books designed to introduce students to the complex world of words that the English language has to offer. Harder to find, however, are resources that show students how and when to use those words correctly. *101 Lessons: Vocabulary Words in Context* takes the learning process that one step further by giving students the more complete comprehension they need in order to accurately use over 500 vocabulary words in their writing and speech.

Lessons 1–74 in this book incorporate at least five vocabulary words, while Lesson 75–101 each include six. Each of the 101 lessons in this book is comprised of three parts:

Section I: Context

The first section of each lesson features a written piece that contains the vocabulary words. Because the words fit comfortably within the context of the piece, students are able to see an example of the correct usage of each word.

Several different written formats are used in this section. One piece may be in the form of a newspaper article, while the next is in that of an informal e-mail. The lessons span the genres, with nonfiction accounts of the extraordinary included alongside fictitious tales of the everyday. In this way, students are able to better understand all of the contexts in which words and language are employed.

In this first section, students participate in the piece in one of two ways:

1. Students are given a list of definitions in a **Definitions Box** and asked to match the correct definition with its corresponding words in the piece. Students must use context clues from the piece to determine which definition fits which word.

2. Students are given a **Mini Dictionary**, a list of vocabulary words and their definitions. The students are then asked to complete the piece by using those words to fill in the blanks. In this type of exercise, students need to understand the context in order to plug in the correct words.

Section II: Repetition

The second section of the book gives students a chance to practice the spelling of their new vocabulary words. Students rewrite each word three times. This repetition gives students a sense of familiarity with the words and helps them commit the words to memory.

Section III: Reinforcement

The third section features an activity that reinforces students' understanding of the words. This section offers several formats, including analogies, context clues, fill-in-the-blanks, matching, synonyms and antonyms, etc.

For ease of use, an answer key is provided on pages 106–109. Also, a complete index of the vocabulary words taught in this book is given on pages 110–112.

Where the Tall Buildings Are

Directions: Find the meaning of each underlined word in the piece. Put the letter of the answer on the blank line. Use the definitions box below to help you.

> A. the number of people living in a particular area
> B. having or containing a lot of people
> C. beyond normal human abilities
> D. a very tall building
> E. an area outside of a city with houses

1. _____
2. _____
3. _____
4. _____
5. _____

Have you ever been up in a ¹skyscraper? If you have, you were in a city and not in the ²suburbs. That's because the biggest buildings are always built in areas where the ³population is the highest—which is in cities. There is no need for such seemingly ⁴superhuman projects in areas that are less ⁵populous. But where there are the most people, there needs to be the most places to work and live. That's why the tallest buildings are not spread out evenly all over a state or country, but are always clumped together in cities.

Directions: Spell each new word three times.

1. skyscraper _____ _____ _____

2. suburbs _____ _____ _____

3. population _____ _____ _____

4. superhuman _____ _____ _____

5. populous _____ _____ _____

Activity: Put your new words in ABC order. Then, next to each word, write the meaning.

1. _____ _____
2. _____ _____
3. _____ _____
4. _____ _____
5. _____ _____

All You Can Eat

Directions: Read the following newspaper advertisement. Use the mini dictionary to help you fill in the missing words.

> **waffle**—a small, crisp cake made from batter (often served with syrup and/or fruit)
> **cheeseburger**—a circle of ground beef with cheese on top served inbetween buns
> **pineapple**—a large, sweet tropical fruit
> **brunch**—a late-morning meal that is a combination of "breakfast" and "lunch"
> **gargantuan**—huge

HAVE A (1.) _____ MEAL FOR JUST $11.95!

Here at Large Tony's, we don't serve breakfast, lunch, or dinner—just
(**2.**) _____. We are open from 10:30 a.m. until 1:30 p.m.
every day, and we offer the most food in the world. Want a
(**3.**) _____ with 22 kinds of syrup, whip cream, and
chocolate sauce? You can get it here! Want a (**4.**) _____
with ketchup, mustard, barbecue sauce, and 12 different cheeses on a
whole wheat bun? Come on down! Want a fruit salad with only big, juicy fruits—
like watermelon, cantaloupe, and (**5.**) _____ ? It's waiting for you
here! Eat as much as you want for $11.95. You'll find no better deal! Eat until you
explode—we don't care! Large Tony is waiting for you!

Directions: Spell each new word three times.

1. waffle _____ _____ _____

2. cheeseburger _____ _____ _____

3. pineapple _____ _____ _____

4. brunch _____ _____ _____

5. gargantuan _____ _____ _____

Activity: Write three sentences of your own. Use two new words in each sentence.

1. _____

2. _____

3. _____

For the Winner

Directions: Find the meaning of each underlined word in the e-mail message below. Put the letter of the answer on the blank line. Use the definitions box to help you.

> A. a substance that is usually shiny, hard, bendable, and can carry heat and electricity
> B. victory, success
> C. having or being many colors
> D. a statue given as a prize
> E. the chief official at a school

1. _____
2. _____
3. _____
4. _____
5. _____

To: trophytime@business.com
From: principal@sierravista.edu
Subject: **making an award**

Hello. I am [1]principal of Sierra Vista Elementary School, and I am hoping your company can make for us a [2]trophy for the winner of our spelling bee. We would like it to be made of whatever silver [3]metal is cheapest, and we would like it to be covered with a [4]multicolored variety of stones. I am hoping you can make it so neat that the winner of the spelling bee will relive his or her [5]triumph every time he or she looks at it. Please e-mail me back with your ideas. Thanks.

Sally Marconi, Sierra Vista Elementary

Directions: Spell each new word three times.

1. principal   _____   _____   _____
2. trophy   _____   _____   _____
3. metal   _____   _____   _____
4. multicolored   _____   _____   _____
5. triumph   _____   _____   _____

Activity: Fill in the blanks below with the new vocabulary words that fit best.

1. I'm so excited! They announced that they're giving a huge _____ to the winner of this year's vocabulary contest!
2. In the first Super Bowl, the Green Bay Packers were able to _____ over the Kansas City Chiefs 35–10.
3. The _____ called a meeting to discuss school policies.
4. My cousin just painted his car purple with _____ spots all over roof. I think it looks very silly.
5. The raindrops made "Ping! Ping!" noises every time they hit the _____ roof of my uncle's cabin.

Setting an Example

Directions: Read the following short piece. Use the mini dictionary to help you fill in the missing words.

> **leadership** — the quality of being a leader
> **jittery** — nervous and jumpy
> **endanger** — to put in danger
>
> **panic** — to become too scared to think clearly
> **mettle** — courage, bravery

In the military, some people are in (**1.**) _____ positions, and those below them must follow their orders. These leaders have a great responsibility. Sometimes they will have to lead their troops into risky situations, but they must be sure not to (**2.**) _____ their troops for no reason. Also, they must never (**3.**) _____ . They must set an example for their troops by showing their (**4.**) _____ . Because of this, someone who is (**5.**) _____ will probably not be a good leader.

Directions: Spell each new word three times.

1. leadership   _____   _____   _____

2. jittery   _____   _____   _____

3. endanger   _____   _____   _____

4. panic   _____   _____   _____

5. mettle   _____   _____   _____

Activity: Decide if the following pairs are synonyms or antonyms. Write **S** (for *synonym*) or **A** (for *antonym*) on each line.

1. panic   calm   _____

2. mettle   cowardice   _____

3. jittery   anxious   _____

4. endanger   protect   _____

5. leadership   guidance   _____

The Wild West in Wisconsin

Directions: Find the meaning of each underlined word in the passage below. Put the letter of the answer on the blank line. Use the definitions box to help you.

> A. to move violently about
> B. to take pictures with a camera
> C. very angry
> D. to breathe in sharply (as in shock)
> E. a sports event featuring the riding and roping of ranch animals

1. _____

2. _____

3. _____

4. _____

5. _____

I was excited when my school newspaper chose me to cover the [1]rodeo that came to our city. We don't have a lot of cowboys here in Green Bay, Wisconsin, so this was a big deal! The paper gave me a camera with which to [2]photograph the things I saw. I was mostly interested in taking pictures of this big bull they had. I thought bulls looked mad on TV, but you should have seen how [3]enraged this one looked! That didn't stop an old cowboy named Tex, though. He climbed onto the bull and got ready to ride. When the gate opened, that bull started to [4]thrash around, trying to get Tex off of his back. It was really exciting! The crowd let out a [5]gasp when Tex finally was thrown off. He hit the ground hard, but he got up quickly to show that he wasn't hurt. Still, I wouldn't want to try riding that bull!

Directions: Spell each new word three times.

1. rodeo   _____   _____   _____

2. photograph   _____   _____   _____

3. enraged   _____   _____   _____

4. thrash   _____   _____   _____

5. gasp   _____   _____   _____

Activity: Write three sentences of your own. Use two new words in each sentence.

1. _____

2. _____

3. _____

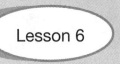

My Least Favorite Place

Directions: Find the meaning of each underlined word in the story below. Put the letter of the answer on the blank line. Use the definitions box to help you.

> A. uncomfortable, anxious
> B. frightened scream
> C. shake, tremble
> D. a room directly below the roof of a building
> E. having no light

1. _____

2. _____

3. _____

4. _____

5. _____

I'll tell you this: I will never go up in the ¹attic of our house again! There are no windows up there, and the light switch isn't even close to the door. Being in that kind of ²darkness—even if it's only for a few seconds— makes me very ³uneasy. So of course my mom sent me up there the other day to get something for her. I had just closed the door behind me when I heard a very scary creaking sound. I was so freaked out, I started to ⁴shiver. Another sound. Whatever it was, it sounded like it was coming toward me and then backing away again. "Hello?" I said. No answer, just that sound again. I had to stop myself from letting out a ⁵shriek. I was shaking as I reached for the light switch. Creak! Creak! I hit the switch.

It was my cat, Sadie, rolling around on an old rocking chair. Who knows what it could have been, though. I'm not taking any chances!

Directions: Spell each new word three times.

1. attic   _____   _____   _____
2. darkness   _____   _____   _____
3. uneasy   _____   _____   _____
4. shiver   _____   _____   _____
5. shriek   _____   _____   _____

Activity: In the following groups of words, circle the one that doesn't belong.

1. uneasy	nervous	calm	restless
2. shiver	shudder	quiver	dance
3. darkness	brightness	glow	shine
4. shriek	speak	screech	squeal
5. attic	kitchen	table	bathroom

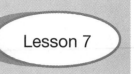

If At First You Don't Succeed...

Directions: Read the following nonfiction piece about a great baseball player. Use the mini dictionary to help you fill in the missing words.

> **mitt** — a glove used to catch a baseball   **pain** — hurt, suffering
>
> **task** — chore, duty   **wild** — untamed, out of control
>
> **career** — a job one does for many years

For the first few years of his baseball (**1.**) _____, Sandy Koufax was not a very good pitcher. He threw the ball very hard, but his pitches were often (**2.**) _____, and they didn't always make it to his catcher's (**3.**) _____. His team, the Brooklyn Dodgers, knew that Koufax had a lot of talent, so they stuck with him. After a few years, the left-handed Koufax learned to control his pitches. Soon, the hitters he faced found hitting his pitches to be an almost impossible (**4.**) _____. Most people would agree that Koufax was the best pitcher in baseball from 1961 to 1966. Unfortunately, his prized left arm had been hurting him for years. After the 1966 season, Koufax was forced to retire because of the terrible (**5.**) _____ in his arm. He was still young when he left the game, but he will always be remembered for working so hard to become one of the greatest of all time.

Directions: Spell each new word three times.

1. mitt _____ _____ _____

2. task _____ _____ _____

3. career _____ _____ _____

4. pain _____ _____ _____

5. wild _____ _____ _____

Activity: Draw a line to match each new word with the idea that best describes it.

1. mitt   A. several years doing the same work

2. task   B. a very unpleasant feeling

3. career   C. this protects your hand

4. pain   D. a difficult thing to do

5. wild   E. unpredictable

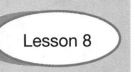

Geography Test on Tuesday

Directions: Find the meaning of each underlined word in the story below. Put the letter of the answer on the blank line. Use the definitions box to help you.

> A. the people who rule a country, city, etc.
> B. book of maps
> C. city or town where the rulers work from
> D. test of knowledge
> E. to study or examine again

1. _____

Ms. Anderson: "Hello, Class. "I hope that all of you had fantastic weekends. But it's back to business! In fact, we'll be having a little test tomorrow."

2. _____

(Class groans.)

3. _____

Ms. Anderson: "It's true. But the good news is that today we will have a full ¹review so you'll know what to expect. The ²exam will cover everything we've learned about the United States this year. You will need to be able to name all three branches of the U.S. ³government and what

4. _____

each of them does. You will need to know the ⁴capital of the U.S., and you will need to locate it on a map. And no, you will not be permitted to use

5. _____

an ⁵atlas to help you. It will take some studying, but I trust you will all do very well."

Directions: Spell each new word three times.

1. review _____ _____ _____
2. exam _____ _____ _____
3. government _____ _____ _____
4. capital _____ _____ _____
5. atlas _____ _____ _____

Activity: Put your new words in ABC order. Then, next to each word, use the word in a sentence.

1. _____ _____
2. _____ _____
3. _____ _____
4. _____ _____
5. _____ _____

Loosen Up For Less!

Directions: Find the meaning of each underlined word in the advertisement below. Put the letter of the answer on the blank line. Use the definitions box to help you.

> A. a snack food shaped like a loose knot
> B. an artistic style of dance
> C. an athletic instructor
> D. able to bend easily
> E. moving with ease and charm

GET YOURSELF TO "A HEALTHY PLACE"

1. _____
2. _____
3. _____
4. _____
5. _____

Have you always wanted to master the [1]graceful art of [2]ballet? Do you dream of being completely [3]flexible and able to twist your body into the shape of a [4]pretzel? You can do all of this and more! Just visit us at our website and we'll have you meeting with your very own personal fitness [5]trainer in no time. And best of all, your first session is free! Come loosen up with us — you'll feel great and you'll save money doing it!

Directions: Spell each new word three times.

1. graceful _____ _____ _____

2. ballet _____ _____ _____

3. flexible _____ _____ _____

4. pretzel _____ _____ _____

5. trainer _____ _____ _____

Activity: Write the best new word in the blank for each idea.

1. I can touch my toes. _____

2. I like salt and mustard on mine. _____

3. I do this to classical music. _____

4. This person helps me at the gym. _____

5. I glide through the air like a bird. _____

Lesson 10

A Concerned Neighbor

Directions: Read the following letter and fill in the blanks with new vocabulary words. Use the mini dictionary to help you.

> **vandal** — one who destroys the property of others
> **kindergarten** — a school or class for young children
> **prank** — trick, joke (often mean-spirited)
>
> **squirm** — wriggle, twist uncomfortably
> **misbehave** — disobey, do bad things

Dear Mr. and Mrs. Goodson:

I don't know how to say it nicely; your son, Victor, has not been a very good boy lately. I have told you this before, but he continues to (**1.**) _____. The other day I caught him turning bugs on their backs and watching them (**2.**) _____. A (**3.**) _____ like that shows that he's a mean boy. Then I saw him draw all over Mrs. Puckett's shiny new mailbox. I worry that he's becoming a (**4.**) _____! I write this to you now because I know that your son will be starting school next month. I feel sorry for his (**5.**) _____ teacher.

Sincerely,

Thelma Looben

Directions: Spell each new word three times.

1. vandal _____ _____ _____

2. kindergarten _____ _____ _____

3. prank _____ _____ _____

4. squirm _____ _____ _____

5. misbehave _____ _____ _____

Activity: Write three sentences. In each sentence, use two of your new words.

1. _____

2. _____

3. _____

A House with a View

Directions: Find the meaning of each underlined word in the piece below. Put the letter of the answer on the blank line. Use the definitions box to help you.

> A. the side of a hill
> B. empty, not occupied
> C. a room or area below a house
> D. very large, gigantic
> E. a room where vehicles are stored

1. _____

2. _____

3. _____

4. _____

5. _____

When my best friend Juan told me that his family was moving, I was not happy. But now that I've seen his new house, I can't wait to visit every day! It's this enormous three-story mansion that sits on a ¹hillside overlooking a beautiful park. And speaking of large, the ²garage is ³mammoth. It can hold up to three cars easily, which is good since Juan will be getting his driver's license in a few years. Also, the house has this cool, underground ⁴cellar. Juan's mom said that they might make a game room down there. What a house! I can't believe how lucky they were that it was ⁵vacant. Oh, and it's only a few blocks further than his old house.

Directions: Spell each new word three times.

1. hillside   _____   _____   _____

2. garage   _____   _____   _____

3. mammoth   _____   _____   _____

4. cellar   _____   _____   _____

5. vacant   _____   _____   _____

Activity: Write the best new word in the blank for each idea.

1. nobody lives here   _____

2. you park your truck here   _____

3. coming down the mountain   _____

4. take the stairs down to go here   _____

5. this is bigger than you   _____

Summer Bake Sale

Directions: Read the following piece about an upcoming event. Use the mini dictionary to help you fill in the missing words.

> **marina** — a water area where small boats dock
> **overcast** — cloudy, gloomy
> **annual** — happening once every year
>
> **pecan** — a type of nut
> **proceeds** — money collected from a fundraiser

Yes, folks, it's that time of year again! Time for the (**1.**) _____ bake sale that is held down by the (**2.**) _____ every July 4th. Just look for all of the boats, and you'll find it. Remember how delicious all of the baked goods were last year? Remember when Mr. Ben Stern's (**3.**) _____ pie won first place? Well, he's back again this year. And if you don't like nuts, don't worry; there will be plenty of other treats. Best of all, the (**4.**) _____ from this year's sale will be used to keep our wonderful town clean and safe. And while the weather report says that the 4th will be an (**5.**) _____ day, we aren't expecting rain. So come on down and bring your appetites!

Directions: Spell each new word three times.

1. marina _____ _____ _____

2. overcast _____ _____ _____

3. annual _____ _____ _____

4. pecan _____ _____ _____

5. proceeds _____ _____ _____

Activity: In each group, cross out the word that doesn't belong.

1. marina   harbor   ocean   bay

2. pecan   berry   walnut   cashew

3. annual   calendar   daily   hourly

4. overcast   clear   sunny   raincoat

5. proceeds   profits   losses   sales

Around the World and Back Again

Directions: Find the meaning of each underlined word in the nonfiction piece below. Put the letter of the answer on the blank line. Use the definitions box to help you.

> A. oldest
> B. accomplishment
> C. trip, journey
> D. to move in a path around a planet or other object
> E. a government worker who represents an area's citizens

1. _____

2. _____

3. _____

4. _____

5. _____

Do you know that John Glenn was the first American to [1]orbit Earth? In 1962 he accomplished this [2]feat by flying a spacecraft called *Friendship* 7 around Earth three times. Much later, in 1998, Glenn became the [3]eldest person to go on a space [4]voyage when he flew on the space shuttle *Discovery*. For most of the 36 years between these two space missions, Glenn was a [5]politician. He was a U.S. senator from the state of Ohio. All in all, John Glenn has been a national hero for a very long time.

Directions: Spell each new word three times.

1. orbit _____ _____ _____

2. feat _____ _____ _____

3. eldest _____ _____ _____

4. voyage _____ _____ _____

5. politician _____ _____ _____

Activity: Fill in the blanks in each sentence with the new word that fits the best.

1. The president of the United States is the country's most powerful _____.

2. The spacecraft was designed to _____ Mars and take photographs of the planet's surface.

3. For our summer vacation, we took a _____ on a cruise ship to Alaska.

4. Now that our _____ brother has his driver's license, he has to drive Annie and me to school.

5. Scoring three goals in one game is a very difficult _____. My dad said it's called a "hat trick" when you do that.

Too Much Fun in the Sun

Directions: Read the following piece. Use the mini dictionary to help you fill in the missing words.

> **kayak** — a small canoe
> **collapse** — fall down
> **navigate** — ride around, sail
>
> **muscles** — parts of the body that are used for movement and strength
> **exhausted** — very tired, fatigued

What a day! All of the (**1.**) _____ in my back and arms ache! I'm not moving from my bed for the rest of the week, I tell you!

It started at 8:00 A.M. this morning — which is way too early if you ask me. It was my cousin's idea to take the (**2.**) _____ out on the river behind our cabin. We must have been paddling around out there for hours in the hot sun. I was totally (**3.**) _____ by about 9:30, but we stayed out on the lake until almost noon. At one point we had to (**4.**) _____ _____ around a big pile of logs that were floating in the river. That did me in. By the time we got home, I was ready to (**5.**) _____ on my bed and go to sleep.

Directions: Spell each new word three times.

1. kayak   _____   _____   _____

2. collapse   _____   _____   _____

3. navigate   _____   _____   _____

4. muscles   _____   _____   _____

5. exhausted   _____   _____   _____

Activity: Write the letter of the best new word on the blank next to the idea it best matches.

_____ 1. The bigger these are, the stronger a person is.   A. kayak

_____ 2. Use this to move down a stream.   B. collapse

_____ 3. Do this when you are tired.   C. navigate

_____ 4. Do this when you are moving along the water.   D. muscles

_____ 5. You feel this way when you've worked too hard.   E. exhausted

Rules of the Road

Directions: Find the meaning of each underlined word in the piece below. Put the letter of the answer on the blank line. Use the definitions box to help you.

> A. absolutely necessary
> B. environment, area around you
> C. command, control
> D. tired, sleepy
> E. follow, do as others do

1. _____
2. _____
3. _____
4. _____
5. _____

"Listen up, people. Many of you are here because you have been caught breaking the rules of the road. That cannot be allowed. If you want to drive a car, it is very important that you [1]conform to certain rules and laws. You can't go too fast. You have to come to a complete stop at stop signs. It is [2]essential that you are aware of your [3]surroundings at all times. In order to [4]helm a motor vehicle, you have to be awake and alert. You cannot be [5]drowsy. You cannot be focused on other things. A car can be very dangerous if its driver is not paying attention."

Directions: Spell each new word three times.

1. conform   _____   _____   _____

2. essential   _____   _____   _____

3. surroundings _____   _____   _____

4. helm   _____   _____   _____

5. drowsy   _____   _____   _____

Activity: On the blank line, write the best new word for each idea.

1. I'm in charge of flying this plane.   _____

2. I'm ready for bed.   _____

3. I'm going to do what everyone else is doing.   _____

4. I must study if I want to get an "A" on the test.   _____

5. I live in a big city that has tall buildings.   _____

Babies Everywhere!

Directions: Read the following piece about animal babies. Use the mini dictionary to help you fill in the missing words.

> **cygnet** — a baby swan   **infant** — a baby gorilla or a very young child
> **fawn** — a baby deer   **offspring** — children (of parents)
> **foal** — a baby horse

It's true, every type of animal has babies. But do you know the names we call each of those different babies? They're not all called children or kids, that's for sure. While a baby gorilla is called an (**1.**) _____ , we have much different names for the (**2.**) _____ of other animals. A baby swan, for instance, is called a (**3.**) _____ . Do you know what a baby horse is called? A (**4.**) _____ . How about a baby deer? That's a (**5.**) _____ . The list goes on and on. If you ever want to know the names of all of the animal babies, you can find that information on the Internet. A good place to look is *http://www.abcteach.com/ abclists/animalbabies.htm*.

Directions: Spell each new word three times.

1. cygnet _____ _____ _____

2. fawn _____ _____ _____

3. foal _____ _____ _____

4. infant _____ _____ _____

5. offspring _____ _____ _____

Activity: Write the best new word in the blank for each idea.

1. will grow up to be a big ape _____

2. will grow up to live in a forest _____

3. will grow up to live in a lake _____

4. will grow up to live on a ranch _____

5. might grow up to look like its parents _____

A Stinging Lesson

Directions: Read the following piece. Use the mini dictionary to help you fill in the missing words.

> **lawn** — ground covered with grass
> **curious** — interested
> **disturb** — annoy, agitate
> **furious** — angry, very mad
>
> **beehive** — a natural structure in which bees live

I've done it this time. I've really made my mother and father (**1.**)_____!
It all started with this (**2.**) _____ that was hanging from a tree
on our front (**3.**) _____ . My parents warned me not to
(**4.**) _____ it. But I was just so (**5.**) _____ !
I tried to knock it down and next thing I knew, there were bees everywhere! I
must have gotten stung at least 10 times! That hurt a lot — but not as much as
the look on my mom's face did. I guess I learned my lesson the hard way.

Directions: Spell each new word three times.

1. lawn _____ _____ _____

2. disturb _____ _____ _____

3. furious _____ _____ _____

4. beehive _____ _____ _____

5. curious _____ _____ _____

Activity: In each group, cross out the word or words that do not belong.

1. furious	unhappy	upset	pleased
2. beehive	dog collar	spider web	anthill
3. lawn	sidewalk	driveway	street
4. disturb	ignore	neglect	leave alone
5. curious	uninterested	intrigued	fascinated

The Not-So-Bad School

Directions: Find the meaning of each underlined word in the e-mail below. Put the letter of the answer on the blank line. Use the definitions box to help you.

> A. school work intended to be completed at home
>
> B. an outfit that shows the wearer belongs to a certain group
>
> C. to sleep, to doze
>
> D. quickly
>
> E. give out, appoint (as to a duty)

To: jennaroo1995@msn.com

From: qtprincessa@yahoo.com

Subject: **worst school ever!!!**

1. _____

2. _____

3. _____

4. _____

5. _____

Yuck!!! My first day was the worst. I miss you guys so much!!! Did I tell you that we have to wear a school [1]uniform? It's really plain and ugly and has NO style. But I do get ready a lot more [2]rapidly in the morning.... Oh, and the amount of [3]homework my teachers [4]assign is ridiculous!

So I guess I'm making new friends at this school. But it's not the same without you and everybody else. I did get invited to a [5]slumber party this weekend, though. Should I go?

You're the best friend ever!

Directions: Spell each new word three times.

1. uniform   _____   _____   _____
2. rapidly   _____   _____   _____
3. homework   _____   _____   _____
4. assign   _____   _____   _____
5. slumber   _____   _____   _____

Activity: Put your new words in ABC order. Then, on the blank line next to each word, use the word in a sentence.

1. _____   _____
2. _____   _____
3. _____   _____
4. _____   _____
5. _____   _____

Two Words in One

Some words look just like two separate words that have been pushed together. That's exactly what they are, and they're called *compound words*.

Directions: Read the statements below. Underline the compound word in each.

1. The largest waterfall in the world is Victoria Falls in Africa.

2. The scorekeeper accidentally awarded the home team with two extra points.

3. Susan wore a long evening gown, and I wore a turtleneck sweater.

4. We took the rowboat out on the lake and fished for hours.

5. Mom and Irene watched Isaac play with the other children in the local park's sandbox.

Directions: Spell each of these compound words three times.

1. railroad _____ _____ _____

2. playground _____ _____ _____

3. spaceship _____ _____ _____

4. lunchtime _____ _____ _____

5. hairbrush _____ _____ _____

Activity: Create five new sentences on the lines below. In each sentence, use at least two compound words.

1. _____

2. _____

3. _____

4. _____

5. _____

Sounds Like Spring

Directions: Read the following story. Use the mini dictionary to fill in the missing words.

> **chirp** — a high-pitched sound
> **eyesight** — vision
> **rustle** — to move with soft crackling or fluttering sounds
>
> **contentment** — satisfaction, happiness
> **limbs** — large tree branches

Springtime has always been Grandma's favorite time of year. She likes to sit out on her front porch and soak in the sounds of nature. Grandma's **(1.)** _____ has not been very good for years, but her hearing is as sharp as ever. In the trees in front of Grandma's house, tiny birds gather on the **(2.)** _____ , and they **(3.)** _____ from sunrise to sunset. When the night comes and the birds stop singing, Grandma likes to listen to the **(4.)** _____ of the wind through the leaves. She says that listening to the sounds of nature brings her a feeling of **(5.)** _____ .

Directions: Spell each new word three times.

1. chirp _____ _____ _____

2. eyesight _____ _____ _____

3. rustle _____ _____ _____

4. contentment _____ _____ _____

5. limbs _____ _____ _____

Activity: An analogy is a comparison between two groups of things. Use what you know of your vocabulary words to fill in the analogies below.

1. _____ is to eyes as hearing is to ears.

2. _____ are to trees as arms are to people.

3. _____ is to movement as sour is to taste.

4. _____ is to birds as bark is to dogs.

5. _____ is to unhappiness as on is to of.

A Great Place to Visit

Directions: Find the meaning of each underlined word in the newspaper article below. Put the letter of the answer on the blank line. Use the definitions box to help you.

A. to change or alter

B. people who visit a place

C. covered with a hard, smooth surface (such as concrete)

D. the place to which people go

E. not necessary, but very comfortable and expensive

MAYOR TO IMPROVE PARADISE

1. _____

2. _____

3. _____

4. _____

5. _____

Paradise, UT — Mayor Kathy Korbett announced plans today to boost Paradise's appeal to ¹tourists. "We would like to ²transform our lovely city into a place that will become an exciting ³destination for people from all over this great state. We've got a lot to offer now, and we'll have even more to offer soon." Mayor Korbett's new vision for the city includes four new restaurants, a ⁴luxurious high-rise hotel, and several freshly ⁵paved parking lots. Some of Paradise's citizens are not pleased with the development. "Paradise was just fine before the mayor started getting ideas," said Daniel Markman, 68, a retired firefighter.

Directions: Spell each new word three times.

1. tourists _____ _____ _____

2. transform _____ _____ _____

3. destination _____ _____ _____

4. luxurious _____ _____ _____

5. paved _____ _____ _____

Activity: Circle the answer that best answers this question: Which word describes . . .

1. the softest quilt in the world? **paved** or **luxurious**

2. visitors to the Grand Canyon? **tourists** or **transform**

3. a new highway? **paved** or **transform**

4. a trip to New York City? **paved** or **destination**

5. a caterpillar becoming a butterfly? **luxurious** or **transform**

Doing the Impossible

Directions: Find the meaning of each underlined word in the nonfiction piece below. Put the letter of the answer on the blank line. Use the definitions box to help you.

> A. raised upright
> B. up-to-date, of the present
> C. a structure built as a memorial
> D. a location
> E. things that are not fully understood

1. _____

2. _____

3. _____

4. _____

5. _____

In the countryside in England there exists one of the world's greatest [1]mysteries. It is called Stonehenge, and it is a huge [2]monument of standing stones that was built over 4,000 years ago. One of the biggest puzzles about Stonehenge is who [3]erected the stones and how they did it. The stones that make up Stonehenge are so gigantic that it doesn't seem possible that they could have been raised without the help of [4]modern machines. Some of the largest stones were even brought to the Stonehenge [5]site from hundreds of miles away! Scientists continue to study Stonehenge in the hope that we may one day fully understand how it came to be. For now though, many questions remain.

Directions: Spell each new word three times.

1. mysteries   _____   _____   _____

2. monument   _____   _____   _____

3. erected   _____   _____   _____

4. modern   _____   _____   _____

5. site   _____   _____   _____

Activity: Look at the following clues. On the line next to each, write the vocabulary word that best fits.

1. something that is new   _____

2. things that are built up   _____

3. unsolved crimes   _____

4. an important place to visit   _____

5. a page on the Internet   _____

A Much Nicer Job

Directions: Find the meaning of each underlined word in the piece below. Put the letter of the answer on the blank line. Use the definitions box to help you.

> A. task, job
> B. fix
> C. to contend with another
>
> D. ready to be used
> E. a state of ease or well-being

1. _____
2. _____
3. _____
4. _____
5. _____

Usually, I spend my summer vacation outdoors, mowing lawns in the hot sun. That's hard work, and I have to [1]<u>compete</u> for jobs with my neighbor Kenny. This year I had a different plan: fixing computers. I made a nice sign that announced that I was [2]<u>available</u> for summer work. Within a few hours, I got four phone calls! It seems that all of my neighbors have computers, but none of them know how to [3]<u>repair</u> them! This latest [4]<u>undertaking</u> of mine pays a lot better than mowing lawns. And best of all, I get to do my job in the [5]<u>comfort</u> of a nice air-conditioned home.

Directions: Spell each new word three times.

1. compete   _____   _____   _____

2. available   _____   _____   _____

3. repair   _____   _____   _____

4. undertaking   _____   _____   _____

5. comfort   _____   _____   _____

Activity: In each group, cross out the word or group of words that doesn't belong. On the blank lines, explain what the remaining group of words have in common.

1. undertaking	activity	thing to do	inactivity	_____
2. repair	break	destroy	damage	_____
3. comfort	luxury	enjoyment	displeasure	_____
4. compete	cooperate	rival	contend	_____
5. available	busy	closed	off limits	_____

My Friend the Entertainer

Directions: Read the paragraph. Use the mini dictionary to help you fill in the missing words.

> **bravo** – an expression of approval
> **performer** – a person who entertains others
> **solo** – an action performed by one person
>
> **anxious** – uneasy, worried
> **vocal** – of the human voice

Yesterday was my best friend Mischa's big night. Her (**1.**) _____
group was singing in front of half of our town; and even though Mischa was on
the stage with everybody else, she had a big (**2.**) _____
that she had to sing all by herself. When it was getting close to her big moment,
I started getting really (**3.**) _____ . But I looked straight at
Mischa and saw that she was as calm as ever. She really loves being on stage—
she's really a fantastic (**4.**) _____ . Once she started to sing, I
relaxed and enjoyed the experience. Her voice is so beautiful! When she was
done, a bunch of us stood up and gave her a huge round of applause. I even
heard some people yelling, "(**5.**) _____ !" I was so happy for
her, she deserved it!

Directions: Spell each new word three times.

1. bravo   _____   _____   _____

2. performer   _____   _____   _____

3. solo   _____   _____   _____

4. anxious   _____   _____   _____

5. vocal   _____   _____   _____

Activity: Put your new words in ABC order. Then, next to each word, write the meaning.

1. _____   _____

2. _____   _____

3. _____   _____

4. _____   _____

5. _____   _____

In the News

Directions: Find the meaning of each underlined word in the newspaper headlines below. Put the letter of the answer on the blank line. Use the definitions box to help you.

> A. recipe, way to make something
> B. marked by courtesy and kindness
> C. weak, not effective
>
> D. help, aid
> E. forbid, prohibit

1. _____ <u>Gracious</u> Lottery Winner Buys New Books for School

2. _____ Falcons Look <u>Feeble</u> in 35-3 Loss to Lions

3. _____ New Law Set to <u>Ban</u> Cell Phone Use in Cars

4. _____ Students to <u>Assist</u> Senior Citizens at Supermarket

5. _____ Secret <u>Formula</u> for Making Famous Soda Revealed

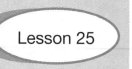

Directions: Spell each new word three times.

1. gracious _____ _____ _____

2. feeble _____ _____ _____

3. ban _____ _____ _____

4. assist _____ _____ _____

5. formula _____ _____ _____

Activity: Write the best new word in the blank in each sentence.

1. We all love Aunt Ginny's super sour lemonade, but she won't let us know the _____ she uses to make it.

2. Our mayor just announced a _____ on the use of camera phones inside all banks and post offices.

3. Several of us stayed after school yesterday to _____ our teacher with the decorations for our classroom's play.

4. In the woods behind our house, my cell phone doesn't work very well. The signal is _____ , and my calls usually get dropped after a minute or two.

5. The loser of the chess championship was very _____ as he shook hands with the winner and gave him a pat on the back.

Rules to Camp By

Directions: Read the sign below. Use the mini dictionary to help you fill in the missing words.

> **container** – something that holds or carries
> **unattended** – not cared for, not paid attention to
> **natural** – produced by nature
>
> **tidy** – neat
> **habitat** – the place in which an animal or plant lives

Welcome Everyone to Camp Sockeye!

We sure hope you enjoy your time here at our campgrounds. Please follow these rules during your stay:

- Do not smoke or leave fires (**1.**) _____. Forest fires are extremely dangerous and can spread very quickly.
- Keep your area clean and (**2.**) _____. If we have to pick up any trash after you leave, you will be charged an extra $20 per night.
- Do not leave an open (**3.**) _____ of food anywhere outside of your tent. No one wants a visit from a bear or other hungry animal!
- No loud music or television at any time. Please enjoy the (**4.**) _____ sights and sounds around you.
- At all times be respectful of the animals and plant life around you. Remember that this is *their* (**5.**) _____, and we are just visitors here.

Thank you, and have a great time!

Directions: Spell each new word three times.

1. container _____ _____ _____
2. unattended _____ _____ _____
3. natural _____ _____ _____
4. tidy _____ _____ _____
5. habitat _____ _____ _____

Activity: Write the best new word in the blank in each sentence.

1. While it may seem too cold to us, the South Pole is the perfect _____ for penguins.
2. Please pick your trash up off the floor and put it in a _____.
3. It is not _____ for people to have bright purple hair.
4. Mom said that if I don't keep my room _____, I won't be allowed to go to the game tomorrow night.
5. It is not a good idea to leave a newborn baby _____ for too long.

A Wonder No More

Directions: Find the meaning of each underlined word in the nonfiction piece below. Put the letter of the answer on the blank line. Use the definitions box to help you.

> A. not often, rarely
> B. obvious, easily seen
> C. not real, not natural
> D. a state of being full of wonder
> E. to leave, to depart from

1. _____

2. _____

3. _____

4. _____

5. _____

When the Astrodome opened in 1965 in Houston, Texas, it was nicknamed "The Eighth Wonder of the World." Why did people feel such [1]amazement toward a building? It was the first domed sports stadium ever, and it was huge. But soon after the dome opened, it became [2]apparent that grass could not survive inside of it. For this reason, a new [3]artificial grass called AstroTurf was invented. AstroTurf looked like grass, but unfortunately, it was much rougher on the athletes who played on it. It was tough on their knees when they ran—and even tougher on their skin when they slid on it.

About 30 years later, two new sports stadiums were built in Houston and the Astrodome was used [4]infrequently. However, in the fall of 2005 the Astrodome did serve an important purpose. At that time, the people who were forced by Hurricane Katrina to [5]evacuate the city of New Orleans came to Houston and lived inside the Astrodome for several weeks. So many people lived inside the Astrodome at that time that it was given its own Zip code—77230—by the U.S. Postal Service.

Directions: Spell each new word three times.

1. amazement _____ _____ _____
2. apparent _____ _____ _____
3. artificial _____ _____ _____
4. infrequently _____ _____ _____
5. evacuate _____ _____ _____

Activity: Put your new words in ABC order. On the line next to each word, use that word in a sentence.

1. _____ _____
2. _____ _____
3. _____ _____
4. _____ _____
5. _____ _____

A Trip Down the Hill

Directions: Read the story below. Use the mini dictionary to help you fill in the missing words.

> **flurry** — a brief, light fall of snow
> **futile** — useless
> **sleigh** — a light vehicle used on ice or snow
> **peak** — the top (as of a mountain or hill)
> **descended** — went down

Annie stood at the (**1.**) _____ of the hill and looked down. An early morning (**2.**) _____ had covered the ground with a fresh blanket of fluffy white snow. She sat down on her (**3.**) _____ and gripped the sides tightly. "Ready!" she yelled, and her friends gave her a strong push. Down the hill Annie raced, gaining speed as she (**4.**) _____ — maybe too much speed! She tried to slow herself down, but it was (**5.**) _____. Just when she thought she'd never stop, the ground grew flat and she started to slow down. Annie laughed as she gently tumbled into a huge pile of snow. From the hill behind her, she could hear her friend Sammy yell out, "My turn!"

Directions: Spell each new word three times.

1. flurry _____ _____ _____

2. futile _____ _____ _____

3. sleigh _____ _____ _____

4. peak _____ _____ _____

5. descended _____ _____ _____

Activity: In the following groups of words, circle the one that doesn't belong.

1. flurry	blizzard	storm	sunshine
2. futile	helpful	effective	useful
3. sleigh	snowmobile	skis	roller skates
4. peak	top	summit	valley
5. descended	fell	went up	came down

Mom's Got Rufus!

Directions: Read the story below. Use the mini dictionary to help you fill in the missing words.

maintain — to keep in good condition	**prefer** — choose, select
lovable — worthy of being loved, inspiring love	**sigh** — to breathe out (with sorrow,
chores — jobs done around the house	surrender, tiredness, or relief)

Every Saturday, my mother hands out the (**1.**) _____ for the week—and not even our Dad can get out of doing something. Now of course, I would (**2.**) _____ to not do anything, but most of the jobs aren't really that horrible.

This week, my mom started off with my dad. She said, "George, it is your duty to (**3.**) _____ the front lawn. It could use a good raking and a mowing." Next, she looked at my sister. "Dishes and trash duty for you." Then she told me to vacuum and dust all of the rooms—which isn't such a bad job to have. "As for me," Mom said as she let out a (**4.**) _____ , "I guess I've got Rufus." "Yay!" we all cheered. Nobody likes picking up after Rufus. He's a (**5.**) _____ pet, but he's a big dog and he makes a big mess!

Directions: Spell each new word three times.

1. maintain _____ _____ _____

2. lovable _____ _____ _____

3. chores _____ _____ _____

4. prefer _____ _____ _____

5. sigh _____ _____ _____

Activity: Put your new words in ABC order. On the line next to each word, use that word in a sentence.

1. _____ _____

2. _____ _____

3. _____ _____

4. _____ _____

5. _____ _____

Finally Found Something

Directions: Find the meaning of each underlined word in the paragraph below. Put the letter of the answer on the blank line. Use the definitions box to help you.

> A. a famous person
> B. listen secretly to a conversation
> C. disappear quickly
> D. interests, activities done for fun
> E. showing skill in the arts

1. _____

2. _____

3. _____

4. _____

5. _____

Over the years, my older brother Shane has had a lot of ¹hobbies. When he was six, he wanted to be a magician. He spent one summer trying to make our pet rabbit ²vanish, but Fluffy never went anywhere. Then Shane wanted to be a "super secret spy." He would sit there for hours with his ear to a fence, trying to ³eavesdrop on our neighbors. They never said anything interesting. When Shane turned 14, he decided he was more of the ⁴artistic type. He started making little movies on our dad's computer. One of his movies won a contest and now he's practically a ⁵celebrity in our town. Maybe he'll stick with this hobby for a while.

Directions: Spell each new word three times.

1. hobbies _____   _____   _____

2. vanish _____   _____   _____

3. eavesdrop _____   _____   _____

4. artistic _____   _____   _____

5. celebrity _____   _____   _____

Activity: Write the best new word in the blank in each sentence.

1. It is not polite to _____ on other people's conversations.

2. When we heard that a famous _____ would be appearing at our school, we couldn't wait to find out who it was.

3. I knew Hailey was _____ but I had no idea she could paint

4. Peter ate so fast that his lunch always seemed to _____ before our eyes.

5. My cousin's two favorite _____ are skateboarding and playing the drums.

Doing Our Part

Directions: Find the meaning of each underlined word in the paragraph below. Put the letter of the answer on the blank line. Use the definitions box to help you.

A. to use again
B. something that is of mixed origins, a combination
C. to let go, to set free

D. affected strongly and favorably
E. something that makes conditions unfit or harmful to living things

1. _____

2. _____

3. _____

4. _____

5. _____

In science class, we were shown a film about ¹pollution and how it hurts the world around us. Our teacher, Mr. Dobbins, asked us to name ways we can help make the air we breathe cleaner. Many students said that their parents drive ²hybrid cars, which run on both gasoline and electricity. Those kinds of cars don't ³release as many bad chemicals into the air. Even more of us said that our families ⁴recycle all of the cans and bottles we use. Mr. Dobbins said he was very ⁵impressed! He said that we can all make a difference, even by doing little things like taking shorter showers and turning off lights when we're not using them.

Directions: Spell each new word three times.

1. pollution _____   _____   _____

2. hybrid _____   _____   _____

3. release _____   _____   _____

4. recycle _____   _____   _____

5. impressed _____   _____   _____

Activity: Write the best new word in the blank in each sentence.

1. I was so _____ with Andrew's ability to throw a baseball.

2. The tire factory was closed down because it caused too much air _____.

3. The scientist invented a way to grow a _____ fruit that is part pear, part pineapple.

4. I caught a really huge fish, but Uncle Tony asked me to _____ it back into the water.

5. The TV critic said that most shows never have any new ideas—they just _____ all of the old ones they've used before.

A Night of Fright

Directions: Read the advertisement below. Use the mini dictionary to help you fill in the missing words.

hoarse — raspy, having a harsh sound
startled — shocked, surprised in a scary way
guarantee — promise, pledge
frightful — causing shock or disgust
yearn — wish for, desire

DEAD HARRY'S SUPER SCARY HAUNTED HOUSE

Do you want to be scared out of your mind?! Do you (**1.**) _____to scream until your voice is (**2.**) _____? Is a (**3.**) _____ evening your idea of a good time? Then you need to run to Dead Harry's Super Scary Haunted House! At Dead Harry's, we (**4.**) _____ that our ghosts, goblins, and ghouls will do the trick. They could jump out at you from anywhere, at anytime. Prepare to be (**5.**) _____!

Directions: Spell each new word three times.

1. hoarse _____ _____ _____

2. startled _____ _____ _____

3. guarantee _____ _____ _____

4. frightful _____ _____ _____

5. yearn _____ _____ _____

Activity: Put your new words in ABC order. On the line next to each word, use that word in a sentence.

1. _____ _____

2. _____ _____

3. _____ _____

4. _____ _____

5. _____ _____

Fast Facts

Directions: Find the meaning of each underlined word in the paragraph below. Put the letter of the answer on the blank line. Use the definitions box to help you.

> A. to remove something from where it grows and plant it in another place
> B. a base or support for an upright structure
> C. making no stops
> D. capable of being carried or moved
> E. one who receives guests

_____ **1.** In 1886 France gave the Statue of Liberty and the <u>pedestal</u> it rests on to the United States as a gift.

_____ **2.** In 1896 Greece became the first country to <u>host</u> the Modern Olympic Games. The Games were also held in Greece in 1906 and 2004.

_____ **3.** In 1954 Joseph Murray performed the first successful <u>transplant</u> of a kidney into a human.

_____ **4.** In 1979—long before there were MP3 Players—the Japanese company Sony invented the Walkman, a <u>portable</u> cassette player.

_____ **5.** In 1988 Kay Cottee became the first female to sail <u>nonstop</u> around the world by herself.

Directions: Spell each new word three times.

1. pedestal _____   _____   _____

2. host _____   _____   _____

3. transplant _____   _____   _____

4. portable _____   _____   _____

5. nonstop _____   _____   _____

Activity: Write the best new word in the blank in each sentence.

1. We took pictures down by the monument's _____ before climbing the stairs up to the top.

2. I took along my _____ television set so I could watch the game on the way to grandmother's house.

3. I wanted to stop somewhere to get something to eat, but Ralph insisted that the trip be _____.

4. Aunt Jo was able to _____ her lemon tree when she moved to the other side of town.

5. Bo's parents let him _____ a swimming party for all of his friends.

City Planning

Directions: Find the meaning of each underlined word in the piece below. Put the letter of the answer on the blank line. Use the definitions box to help you.

> A. a channel that carries water from one place to another
> B. a channel that carries off waste materials
> C. to think about seriously
> D. a technical drawing that shows how to make something
> E. relating to the study of numbers

1. _____

2. _____

3. _____

4. _____

5. _____

Planning and building an entire city isn't easy. There are a lot of things to ^{1}consider. Roads needs to be built, ^{2}sewer systems need to be put in place, and so much more. Is the city located near a water supply? If not, an ^{3}aqueduct will need to be built so that water can be brought in from another area. There are so many questions and a lot of work to be done. How should you begin? The first step might be to draw up a ^{4}blueprint of the city and mark where everything will go. You will need all of those ^{5}mathematical skills you learned in school to do this.

Directions: Spell each new word three times.

1. consider _____ _____ _____

2. sewer _____ _____ _____

3. aqueduct _____ _____ _____

4. blueprint _____ _____ _____

5. mathematical _____ _____ _____

Activity: Put your new words in ABC order. On the line next to each word, use that word in a sentence.

1. _____ _____

2. _____ _____

3. _____ _____

4. _____ _____

5. _____ _____

Peace and Quiet

Directions: Find the meaning of each underlined word in the piece below. Put the letter of the answer on the blank line. Use the definitions box to help you.

> A. loud, harsh noise
> B. easily recognized, unlike any others
> C. seemingly without end
> D. make an effort, concern oneself
> E. marked by chance, hit or miss

1. _____

The Wheltons were a loud family. They lived next door to us for six years, until one day last week when they suddenly moved out.

2. _____

"Movin' to Mississippi," the father, Virgil Whelton, announced; and the next day, the Wheltons were gone.

3. _____

At once, their always-noisy house became quiet. The ¹ceaseless ²din of loud voices and even louder stereo equipment was replaced by silence. The ³haphazard clanging of drum cymbals—Bobby Whelton owned a drum set but could never ⁴bother to take lessons—was not to be heard. At

4. _____

night, we no longer had to listen to the ⁵distinct sound of Ma Whelton's snoring. Nobody else could snore like that!

5. _____

So tonight we decided to stay home and enjoy the peace and quiet. After all, our new neighbors are moving in tomorrow.

Directions: Spell each new word three times.

1. ceaseless   _____   _____   _____
2. din   _____   _____   _____
3. haphazard   _____   _____   _____
4. bother   _____   _____   _____
5. distinct   _____   _____   _____

Activity: Decide if the words on the right are synonyms or antonyms of your new vocabulary words. Write **S** (for *synonym*) or **A** (for *antonym*) in each blank.

1. ceaseless   ending, done, finished   _____
2. din   quiet, peacefulness, calmness   _____
3. haphazard   careless, aimless, by chance   _____
4. bother   ignore, disregard, neglect   _____
5. distinct   clear, definite, well defined   _____

When Given a Chance

Directions: Find the meaning of each underlined word in the nonfiction piece below. Put the letter of the answer on the blank line. Use the definitions box to help you.

> A. give pay to in exchange for work
> B. a member of a group or squad
> C. needed
> D. voted in, chosen
> E. something that stops or restricts

1. _____

2. _____

3. _____

4. _____

5. _____

Marion Motley just wanted a chance to do what he did best: play football. Marion Motley was an African American, and for a long time, no professional football teams wanted to [1]employ African Americans. Finally at the age of 26, Motley was given a chance to try out for one team, the Cleveland Browns. The year was 1946 — one year before Jackie Robinson broke the color [2]barrier in baseball. Motley made the team, and he went on to be one of the greatest players in football history. He was a big, fast, tough runner who led the league in rushing in 1948 and 1950. He was also a great blocker who risked getting hurt in order to protect his team's quarterback. On defense, he was a hard tackler, and the other teams feared him. This was one of the reasons why Motley was known as a great [3]teammate; he would do whatever was [4]necessary to help his team win. And the Browns won a lot! From 1946–1950, the Browns won five straight championships. In 1968, Motley became the second African American to be [5]elected to the Pro Football Hall of Fame.

Directions: Spell each new word three times.

1. employ _____ _____ _____
2. barrier _____ _____ _____
3. teammate _____ _____ _____
4. necessary _____ _____ _____
5. elected _____ _____ _____

Activity: Decide if the following pairs are synonyms or antonyms. Write **S** (for *synonym*) or **A** (for *antonym*) in each blank.

1. employ   hire   _____
2. barrier   opening   _____
3. teammate   enemy   _____
4. necessary   required   _____
5. elected   refused   _____

Art Class

Directions: Find the meaning of each underlined word in the piece below. Put the letter of the answer on the blank line. Use the definitions box to help you.

> A. pointing toward the ground
> B. a soft, dull-gray writing substance
> C. an undetailed drawing
> D. something done to improve a skill
> E. the way a group of things are positioned

1. _____
2. _____
3. _____
4. _____
5. _____

"Hello, everyone, and welcome to the first day of art class. Do you see the [1]arrangement of flowers in the vase on the table at the front of the class? For our first [2]exercise, each of you will create a quick [3]sketch of this object. You will have 10 minutes to complete your drawings, and you will use [4]lead pencils to do them. When you are done, please place your papers [5]facedown on your desks. If you have any questions, please feel free to ask. Alright then, begin."

Directions: Spell each new word three times.

1. arrangement _____ _____ _____

2. exercise _____ _____ _____

3. sketch _____ _____ _____

4. lead _____ _____ _____

5. facedown _____ _____ _____

Activity: Draw lines to connect your new vocabulary words with the ideas on the right.

1. arrangement   A. a thing that's in a pencil but not in a pen

2. exercise   B. a good start, but not a finished painting

3. sketch   C. a way to get better, but not a real test

4. lead   D. a way to look at the floor but not the ceiling

5. facedown   E. a way to put things together, but not a recipe

A Cooked-Up Club

Directions: Read the following piece about this real-life event. Use the mini dictionary to help you fill in the missing words.

> **ingredients** — the things that go into a mixture
>
> **entrée** — the main course of a meal
>
> **counsel** — to give advice
>
> **council** — a group that meets for discussion
>
> **bungalow** — a small one-story house

Notes from the First Ever Meeting of the Clark County Kids Cooking Club

Members of the (**1.**) _____ :

- Janna
- Bobby

- Cecilyn
- Nami

- Devon
- Coby

Things we decided:

- Cecilyn will take notes from each meeting of our cooking club.
- The club will meet once a week in the (**2.**) _____ behind Bobby's parents' house.
- Bobby's mother will (**3.**) _____ us if we have any cooking questions.
- Each club member has to share one recipe (with a complete list of (**4.**) _____) each meeting.
- Each club member will bring one dinner (**5.**) _____ to the once-a-month dinner party at Nami's house.

Directions: Spell each new word three times.

1. ingredients _____ _____ _____

2. entrée _____ _____ _____

3. counsel _____ _____ _____

4. council _____ _____ _____

5. bungalow _____ _____ _____

Activity: Circle the best answer to each of the following phrases.

1. a place to sleep   **council** or **bungalow**
2. a suggestion   **council** or **counsel**
3. flour, sugar, and salt   **ingredients** or **entrée**
4. a steak and a baked potato   **ingredients** or **entrée**
5. a meeting of lawmakers   **council** or **counsel**

An Unforgettable Fire

Directions: Find the meaning of each underlined word in the piece below. Put the letter of the answer on the blank line. Use the definitions box to help you.

> A. a ship's kitchen
> B. a ship that carries goods
> C. a dock or port for ships
>
> D. to hold back, to keep manageable
> E. to get away

1. _____

2. _____

3. _____

4. _____

5. _____

My grandpa always tells the story of the day he was able to [1]escape from a sinking ship. "It began like every other trip. Our [2]freighter had just left the [3]wharf and was floating along nicely. Then suddenly, Arthur the cook came running out of the [4]galley, yelling for help. There was thick, black smoke pouring out of the doorway. We fought that fire with all we had, but we just couldn't [5]contain it. The ship was going down fast! Luckily, we had enough lifeboats for all of us to use, but it was a close call. I'll never forget that day. Even if I could, your grandma wouldn't let me. That was the day I met her! So I guess we can all thank that fire for bringing us together."

Directions: Spell each new word three times.

1. escape   _____   _____   _____

2. freighter   _____   _____   _____

3. wharf   _____   _____   _____

4. galley   _____   _____   _____

5. contain   _____   _____   _____

Activity: Write the best new word in the blank for each idea.

1. what a jug does to water   _____

2. what air does from a leaky tire   _____

3. where a boat might be parked   _____

4. where a dinner might be prepared   _____

5. takes goods from one continent to another   _____

Making the Military

Directions: Find the meaning of each underlined word in the piece below. Put the letter of the answer on the blank line. Use the definitions box to help you.

> A. tiredness
> B. soldier
> C. a school for studying a special skill
> D. to feel sorry for, usually because of feeling the same way
> E. freedom

1. _____

2. _____

3. _____

4. _____

5. _____

One way to become a ¹troop member in one of the armed forces (which are the Army, Navy, Air Force, Marines, Coast Guard, and National Guard) is to go to a military ²academy. There, you will have less ³liberty than you are used to, as people in the military must learn to do exactly what they're told to do. You will have to study hard to graduate, all while doing a lot of physical activity. You will experience a lot of ⁴fatigue. But this will help make you strong. Also, since your classmates will be going through the same things, you will be able to ⁵commiserate with someone. This will help you become close with your fellow future soldiers—something that is very important if you ever go to battle together.

Directions: Spell each new word three times.

1. troop _____ _____ _____

2. academy _____ _____ _____

3. liberty _____ _____ _____

4. fatigue _____ _____ _____

5. commiserate _____ _____ _____

Activity: Put your new words in ABC order. Then, next to each word, write the meaning.

1. _____ _____

2. _____ _____

3. _____ _____

4. _____ _____

5. _____ _____

A Famous Cheater

Directions: Read the following piece about this real-life event. Use the mini dictionary to help you fill in the missing words.

> **infamous** — having a bad reputation; disgraceful
> **marathon** — a 26.2-mile footrace (or anything that lasts a very long time)
> **historic** — very important; history-making
> **invalid** — not legal or allowed
> **foul** — something that is against the rules

The Boston (**1.**) _____ is maybe the world's most famous race. Every year, tens of thousands of people compete, including most of the best long-distance runners in the world. In 1980, Rosie Ruiz was the first woman to cross the finish line. But no one had ever heard of her, and she really didn't look like a runner. Before long, witnesses reported that they saw her take the subway to the end of the race—something that is obviously a (**2.**) _____ . Within a couple of days, her victory was ruled (**3.**) _____ . This was a (**4.**) _____ moment in the history of the race, because it was the first time that something like this had happened. As a result of her cheating, Ruiz is maybe the most (**5.**) _____ person in the history of running.

Directions: Spell each new word three times.

1. infamous   _____   _____   _____
2. marathon   _____   _____   _____
3. historic   _____   _____   _____
4. invalid   _____   _____   _____
5. foul   _____   _____   _____

Activity: Circle the best answer to the following question: Which word describes . . .

1. an act of cheating?   **historic** or **foul**
2. an important event?   **historic** or **invalid**
3. a very long race?   **historic** or **marathon**
4. an unacceptable action?   **marathon** or **invalid**
5. a person who is known for doing something bad?   **infamous** or **foul**

Taking Littering Seriously

Directions: Find the meaning of each underlined word on the sign below posted on every street corner in a city that really wants you to help keep it clean. Put the letter of the answer on the blank line. Use the definitions box to help you.

A. not allowed

B. a place that holds something

C. do not do; avoid

D. splash droplets all over

E. walk

1. _____

2. _____

3. _____

4. _____

5. _____

NOTICE: DO NOT LITTER

All trash must go in a trash ¹receptacle. It is ²prohibited to place trash anywhere else. If a trashcan is full, you must ³troop to another one. You must ⁴abstain from littering, or pay a fine of $100. Gently place in a trashcan any containers with liquid inside. If you throw them and they ⁵splatter, this is considered littering. Please help keep our city beautiful and clean. Thank you.

Directions: Spell each new word three times.

1. receptacle _____ _____ _____

2. prohibited _____ _____ _____

3. troop _____ _____ _____

4. abstain _____ _____ _____

5. splatter _____ _____ _____

Activity: Fill in the blanks in each sentence with the best new word.

1. If you want to lose weight, you should _____ from eating too much fat or sugar.

2. Be careful to not _____ water all over the place when you dive in the pool.

3. We collect our empty cans in a special _____ so that we can recycle them later.

4. After having to _____ three miles up a steep hill, the hikers were ready to rest.

5. Our teacher said that chewing gum is strictly _____ in the classroom.

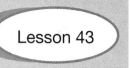

Raising Money on TV

Directions: Read the following piece about something you've probably seen part of on television. Use the mini dictionary to help you fill in the missing words.

> **chitchat** — talk that is casual or unimportant
> **tiresome** — something that makes you bored or tired
> **vaudeville** — entertainment with many different little shows
> **telethon** — a long TV event to get people to call in and donate money
> **bountiful** — plenty

One way to raise money is to put on a (**1.**) _____. Usually these run for many hours—and sometimes as long as days. It would be very (**2.**) _____ to watch the whole thing, but keeping people watching the whole time is not the idea, anyway. There are many different people involved, many (**3.**) _____ acts, and a lot of (**4.**) _____. The hope is that if you stay on TV long enough and tell people about the reason you're putting on the show for them, many people will see a part of it and call in to give money. If you do it right and people want to help, it can prove to be very (**5.**) _____—which sometimes means millions of dollars!

Directions: Spell each new word three times.

1. chitchat _____ _____ _____

2. tiresome _____ _____ _____

3. vaudeville _____ _____ _____

4. telethon _____ _____ _____

5. bountiful _____ _____ _____

Activity: Write the best new word in the blank for each idea.

1. a way to fund research to cure a disease _____

2. waiting in line for an hour at the supermarket _____

3. a large Thanksgiving dinner _____

4. a conversation about how nice the weather is _____

5. a show with a juggler, a singer, and a comedian _____

Hurricane Warning

Directions: Find the meaning of each underlined word in the article below. Put the letter of the answer on the blank line. Use the definitions box to help you.

Definitions Box

A. bumpy, unstable

B. a small group of people living off by themselves

C. a small group of islands

D. the center of a group or organization

E. a device that measures the pressure of the air in the atmosphere

1. _____

2. _____

3. _____

4. _____

5. _____

It was a small country that did not have advanced scientific equipment. It was located in the middle of the ocean, and so it was important to know when hurricanes were coming. They decided to set up a [1]colony of scientists on one of the islands of an [2]archipelago 50 miles to the east. This would be the [3]headquarters for warning the mainland of trouble. The [4]barometer they had there would show the changes that told them a hurricane might be coming before equipment on the mainland would. They would also know when the water was becoming very [5]turbulent while things were still calm on the shores of the rest of the country. With this information, they could use a telephone or radio to warn the citizens to prepare for the hurricane, and so many lives would be saved.

Directions: Spell each new word three times.

1. colony _____ _____ _____

2. archipelago _____ _____ _____

3. headquarters _____ _____ _____

4. barometer _____ _____ _____

5. turbulent _____ _____ _____

Activity: On the blank line, write the best new word for each idea.

1. A club might meet here. _____

2. This helps the weatherman know how humid it is outside. _____

3. A bumpy plane ride could be described this way. _____

4. The Pilgrims set up one of these in America. _____

5. There's one off the coast of Alaska. _____

A Bad Review

Directions: Read the following review of a new computer product. Use the mini dictionary to help you fill in the missing words.

> **modem** — a piece of equipment that allows computers to communicate over telephone lines
>
> **criticism** — finding problems with or fault
>
> **malfunction** — not working correctly
>
> **doodad** — a gadget, usually one that's worthless
>
> **cumbersome** — bulky; of a shape or size that is awkward

THE YOU-COMMUNICATOR 3000

The Communicator 3000 is a (**1.**) _____ this company designs to look just like your head. You send them a picture of you and $499.95, and in a month you get a big package in the mail. I must say, it's very lifelike. However, I have one (**2.**) _____; when you hook it up to your computer, instead of connecting you to the Internet, it's guaranteed to (**3.**) _____ —and you can't connect to anything! What you end up owning is a (**4.**) _____ (**5.**) _____ that's only worth anything if you like looking at your head. Grade: F

Directions: Spell each new word three times.

1. modem _____ _____ _____

2. criticism _____ _____ _____

3. malfunction _____ _____ _____

4. doodad _____ _____ _____

5. cumbersome _____ _____ _____

Activity: Make three new sentences of your own. Use two new words in each sentence.

1. _____

2. _____

3. _____

Poor Little Chicken!

Directions: Find the meaning of each underlined word in the dialog below. Put the letter of the answer on the blank line. Use the definitions box to help you.

> A. not solid, unsteady
> B. a person or animal that is sick or hurt
> C. a type of bird, such as a turkey
> D. feeling bad or sorry for someone
> E. not in the correct shape

1. _____

"Why is that chicken walking so slowly?"

"I don't know."

2. _____

"Oh, look: his right leg is ¹malformed. It's too ²flimsy to fully hold his weight. Poor little ³fowl!"

"It's just a chicken."

3. _____

"But look at him! He's a little ⁴invalid."

"You're so silly."

4. _____

"You don't feel any ⁵sympathy for him?"

"No—it's a chicken. I *eat* chicken."

5. _____

"Yeah, but look at him. Poor little guy."

Directions: Spell each new word three times.

1. malformed _____ _____ _____

2. flimsy _____ _____ _____

3. fowl _____ _____ _____

4. invalid _____ _____ _____

5. sympathy _____ _____ _____

Activity: In the following groups of words, circle the one that doesn't belong.

1. chicken	poultry	salmon	fowl
2. flimsy	stable	solid	steady
3. deformed	malformed	faultless	disfigured
4. strong	healthy	invalid	well
5. sympathy	neglect	pity	understanding

A Number of Jobs

Directions: Read the following employment ad. Use the mini dictionary to help you fill in the missing words.

> **numerator** — the top part of a fraction   **numeral** — number
> **string** — to put together in a line   **compile** — to collect or group together
> **clarity** — clearness

MATH TEACHERS WANTED

Do you like numbers so much that you have a favorite (**1.**) _____?
Do you know a (**2.**) _____ from a denominator? Do you
(**3.**) _____ together numbers just for fun? Do you
(**4.**) _____ your favorite math equations in a scrapbook? Can you
explain formulas with (**5.**) _____? If so, please call
(888) 528-5555, because we need you! One hundred jobs available for math
teachers. Apply now!

Directions: Spell each new word three times.

1. numerator   _____   _____   _____

2. string   _____   _____   _____

3. clarity   _____   _____   _____

4. numeral   _____   _____   _____

5. compile   _____   _____   _____

Activity: Put your new words in ABC order. Then, next to each word, write the meaning.

1. _____   _____

2. _____   _____

3. _____   _____

4. _____   _____

5. _____   _____

A Strange Co-Worker

Directions: Find the meaning of each underlined word in the dialog below. Put the letter of the answer on the blank line. Use the definitions box to help you.

> A. strange, unusual
> B. a person new in something and without experience
> C. a person who works with chemicals and elements
> D. weird, crazy
> E. made up of one syllable

1. _____

2. _____

3. _____

4. _____

5. _____

"That guy is [1]weird. He always wears the same clothes."

"You're just a [2]novice. You'll get used to him.

"Have you noticed that when you ask him a question all of his answers are [3]monosyllabic? 'Yes,' 'no,' 'wrong' . . . It's creepy."

"I like him. His long hair, the way he dances while he's working . . . It makes work more fun."

"I'm going to write a story about him. I'm going to call it 'The [4]Zany [5]Chemist.'"

"I like the title. I can't wait to read it. I already know I'll like the main character."

Directions: Spell each new word three times.

1. weird   _____   _____   _____

2. novice   _____   _____   _____

3. monosyllabic   _____   _____   _____

4. zany   _____   _____   _____

5. chemist   _____   _____   _____

Activity: Fill in the blanks in each sentence with the best new word.

1. "Yes" and "no" are _____ words, but "hello" and "goodbye" are not.

2. My neighbor is a _____ who has been working on a new type of glue.

3. I used to think my English teacher was really _____ but now I think she's normal.

4. Linda's favorite television show is about a _____ fitness instructor who thinks she is from outer space.

5. Right now I'm a _____, so I have to ski on the beginner slopes.

For the Birds

Directions: Read the following newspaper article. Use the mini dictionary to help you fill in the missing words.

skulk — to creep
treacherous — mean and dishonest
abduct — to kidnap

accusation — saying someone did
something bad
blunder — a bad mistake

BIRD THIEF CAUGHT BY SIXTH-GRADER

A man who police say had stolen 20 birds from local pet stores was caught yesterday when a sixth-grade girl, Karynn MacRae, 12, brought her mother over to a cage in Pets-Are-Us to show her a bird she wanted to take home as a pet. However, the bird she had in mind wasn't there. Then she noticed a man in a long coat trying to (**1.**) _____ out the door—and there was something moving in one of the pockets. MacRae figured the man was trying to (**2.**) _____ the bird, and she quickly made her (**3.**) _____ to a security guard, who stopped the man. When questioned, he admitted his crime. "His (**4.**) _____ was that he didn't notice a very smart girl who'd fallen in love with a bird," said Rick Miggly, the security guard who stopped the man.

When police searched the man's home, they found 20 birds, 11 of which were in very poor health. "What makes his crimes extra (**5.**) _____," Miggly said, "was that not only did he steal, he took exotic birds that he didn't know how to care for. They'd have all died if not for Karynn."

Directions: Spell each new word three times.

1. skulk _____ _____ _____
2. treacherous _____ _____ _____
3. abduct _____ _____ _____
4. accusation _____ _____ _____
5. blunder _____ _____ _____

Activity: Put all of your new words in ABC order. Then, next to each word, write the meaning of the word as it's used on this page.

1. _____ _____
2. _____ _____
3. _____ _____
4. _____ _____
5. _____ _____

A Disappointing Event

Directions: Find the meaning of each underlined word in the piece below. Put the letter of the answer on the blank line. Use the definitions box to help you.

> A. a person who goes into outer space
> B. a book written about one's own life
> C. signature; a person writing his or her own name
> D. an abbreviation of "influenza," an illness that usually includes a fever
> E. to mingle or mix with other people

1. _____
2. _____
3. _____
4. _____
5. _____

I've always dreamed of going into space, and people who have done that have always been my heroes. So I was excited when an [1]autobiography by my favorite [2]astronaut was published. I was even more excited when I heard that there would be a book signing by him in my town! This would give me a chance not only to get his [3]autograph on my book, but also to [4]hobnob with one of my heroes. When the day came, I got to the bookstore so early that I was the first person in line. But my day was ruined when the manager of the bookstore came out and told everyone there that the author would not be coming because he had the [5]flu. It just goes to show that even if you've been out of this world, you can still get sick from things on Earth.

Directions: Spell each new word three times.

1. autobiography _____ _____ _____
2. astronaut _____ _____ _____
3. autograph _____ _____ _____
4. hobnob _____ _____ _____
5. flu _____ _____ _____

Activity: Draw lines to connect your new vocabulary words with the ideas on the right.

1. autobiography   A. you stay home sick
2. astronaut   B. you talk to everyone at the party
3. autograph   C. you write your name
4. hobnob   D. you tell your story
5. flu   E. you travel far

Not a Car—but Who Cares?

Directions: Read the following story. Use the mini dictionary to help you fill in the missing words.

> **deli** — short for "delicatessen"; a shop selling meat, cheese, sandwiches, and side dishes
>
> **gym** — short for "gymnasium"; a building for exercise and certain sports
>
> **vet** — short for "veterinarian"; an animal doctor
>
> **gas** — short for "gasoline"; a liquid fuel made from oil that produces energy by burning
>
> **moped** (MO-ped) — a combination of "pedal" and "motorcycle"; a two-wheeled vehicle with both a motor and pedals

I was too young to drive a car, but when I turned 15 my parents bought me a
(**1.**) _____ so that I could drive myself around town. I needed
money for (**2.**) _____, so I got a job working for a (**3.**) _____,
even though I don't really know much about animals. Yesterday I drove down
to the (**4.**) _____ downtown to meet some friends to play basketball, then
I drove to the other side of town to a (**5.**) _____ to meet some other
friends for lunch. It's so great to be able to go all over town. Next year I'll get
my driver's license, but right now I'm so happy with how I can get around that
I'm not even looking forward to it that much.

Directions: Spell each new word three times.

1. deli _____   _____   _____
2. gym _____   _____   _____
3. vet _____   _____   _____
4. gas _____   _____   _____
5. moped _____   _____   _____

Activity: Put your new vocabulary words in alphabetical order. Use each word in a sentence.

1. _____   _____
2. _____   _____
3. _____   _____
4. _____   _____
5. _____   _____

Not Good in Chemistry

Directions: Find the meaning of each underlined word in the progress report below. Put the letter of the answer on the blank line. Use the definitions box to help you.

> A. caring very much about how one looks
> B. an abbreviation of "veteran"; a person with experience in a particular area
> C. one of three basic ways in which all things exist (the others being solid and liquid)
> D. air pollution
> E. one of many tubes in the body that takes blood back to the heart to get oxygen

Progress report for JOHNSON, JIM E.—Chemistry

1. _____
2. _____
3. _____
4. _____
5. _____

This is the third time Jim has taken my chemistry class. However, even though he's a ¹vet in this class, he still doesn't seem to understand the basics. For example, on a recent test, he said that ²smog was a liquid and not a ³gas. One problem seems to be that he is very ⁴vain. I often catch him looking at himself in a mirror. Usually when he does that he flexes his arm and stares at this ⁵vein that pops out. I suggest getting him a tutor to help him with his basic study habits.

Directions: Spell each new word three times.

1. vet _____ _____ _____
2. smog _____ _____ _____
3. gas _____ _____ _____
4. vain _____ _____ _____
5. vein _____ _____ _____

Activity: Draw lines to connect each of the new words below to the idea it matches.

1. vet	A. bad for the environment
2. smog	B. blood moves through it
3. gas	C. very concerned with appearances
4. vain	D. no amateur
5. vein	E. solid, liquid, . . . and this

The Earth of Earth

Directions: Read the following passage. Use the mini dictionary to help you fill in the missing words.

> **geography** — the study of the surface of the Earth
> **geology** — the science of what rocks are made of
> **quicksand** — a loose, wet sand that sucks in anything that falls in it
> **boulder** — a large rock made smooth from wind and water
> **desert** — a dry, sand-covered area of land

The prefix geo- means "land or earth." There are many different things on Earth, and many different parts of Earth's earth to learn about. For example, if you want to know what a (**1.**) _____ is made of, you would study (**2.**) _____ . However, let's say you didn't need to find out what things are made out of but where certain things are on our planet. Where on Earth would you need to watch out for (**3.**) _____ ? Where is the biggest (**4.**) _____ in the world or the tallest mountains? To learn about this, you would study (**5.**) _____ .

Directions: Spell each new word three times.

1. geography   _____   _____   _____
2. geology   _____   _____   _____
3. quicksand   _____   _____   _____
4. boulder   _____   _____   _____
5. desert   _____   _____   _____

Activity: Fill in the blanks with the best new vocabulary word.

1. Luann said that she is really afraid of stepping in _____, but I don't think she'll come across any in the middle of the city.

2. In _____ class we learned that the Sahara is a large _____ that is located in Africa.

3. Bob said, "I don't have to be a professor of _____ to know that this huge _____ is made of rock!"

Cooling Off on Vacation

Directions: Read the following postcard. Use the mini dictionary to help you fill in the missing words.

> **waterfront** — a part of a town that is at the edge of a body of water
>
> **yacht** — a small passenger ship
>
> **sweltering** — very hot
>
> **driftwood** — wood floating on the water
>
> **vessel** — usually a vehicle, but anything that carries something else

Dear Brenda,

Hi! I'm writing to you from our hotel room. I just got back from the neatest cruise! It's (**1.**) _____ here in Southern California. People here tell me it's always like this in July. Anyway, we wanted to cool off, so my mom and dad decided to take me and Dylan down to the (**2.**) _____ , hoping that the breeze coming off the water would be nice. When we got there, we met some nice people who owned a (**3.**) _____ , and they invited us to come onboard. It was a beautiful (**4.**) _____ ! At sunset, we set out. At one point Dylan screamed, thinking we were running into something that was going to sink us, but it was just some (**5.**) _____ . It was funny. Well, I'm going to go to bed now. I hope all is going well with you back in Minnesota. I'll see you in a week or so.

Your friend,

Kelly

Directions: Spell each new word three times.

1. waterfront _____ _____ _____
2. yacht _____ _____ _____
3. sweltering _____ _____ _____
4. driftwood _____ _____ _____
5. vessel _____ _____ _____

Activity: Write three of your own sentences. Include two new vocabulary words in each sentence.

1. _____
2. _____
3. _____

Sightseeing in Washington, D.C.

Directions: Read the following dialogue. Use the mini dictionary to help you fill in the missing words.

> **triangle** — a two-dimensional (or flat) figure with three sides
>
> **octagon** — a two-dimensional figure with eight sides
>
> **pentagon** — a two-dimensional figure with five sides
>
> **polygon** — a two-dimensional figure with many sides
>
> **landmark** — an object in a place that makes it easy to see or remember

"Excuse me, do you live here in Washington? Oh, good. Maybe you can help me. I'm looking for . . . Oh, I can't remember what it's called. It's a big building. It's a . . . (**1.**) _____ or something."

"It's got three sides?"

"No, more than that. It's some sort of (**2.**) _____ —that I'm sure of!"

"But you don't know exactly how many sides?"

"No. Wait. Is there a building that's shaped like an (**3.**) _____ ?"

"Eight sides?"

"No, that's too many. Oh! It's a famous (**4.**) _____ , too! Why can't I remember? Are there any buildings with . . . five sides?"

"Like a (**5.**) _____ ? Yes, there is. That's what it's called, too."

"No wonder I couldn't remember! How do I get there?"

Directions: Spell each new word three times.

1. triangle _____ _____ _____
2. octagon _____ _____ _____
3. pentagon _____ _____ _____
4. polygon _____ _____ _____
5. landmark _____ _____ _____

Activity: Write the letter of the shape below the word it matches.

1. triangle 2. octagon 3. pentagon 4. polygon 5. landmark

____ ____ ____ ____ ____

A. B. C. D. E.

A Poem About Serving Food

Directions: Find the meaning of each underlined word in the poem below. Put the letter of the answer on the blank line. Use the definitions box to help you.

A. belief, opinion
B. nonsense
C. promise, guarantee
D. a five-line poem that rhymes AABBA
E. a type of very good plate

The Way You Want It

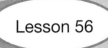

1. _____ I'm writing this ¹limerick about the food that you cook

2. _____ And how rules about serving it are ²gobbledygook

3. _____ So if you ³pledge that nothing is finer

4. _____ Than eating spaghetti on your mother's good ⁴china

5. _____ I think you should give that ⁵notion another look

Directions: Spell each new word three times.

1. limerick   _____ _____ _____

2. gobbledygook   _____ _____ _____

3. pledge   _____ _____ _____

4. china   _____ _____ _____

5. notion   _____ _____ _____

Activity: Put your vocabulary words in ABC order. Use each word in a sentence.

1. _____ _____

2. _____ _____

3. _____ _____

4. _____ _____

5. _____ _____

Under the Big Top

Directions: Read the following piece. Use the mini dictionary to help you fill in the missing words.

> **trampoline** — a strong fabric sheet connected to a frame by strings or springs and used for jumping on
>
> **mare** — a female horse
>
> **unicorn** — a mythical, horse-like animal with a single horn in the middle of its head
>
> **unicycle** — a one-wheeled vehicle with a seat and pedals
>
> **saxophone** — a brass instrument played by blowing into it and fingering its valves

Yesterday I went to the circus for the first time, and I saw some amazing things. There was this clown that did all kinds of tricks in the air while he was jumping on a (**1.**) _____. He even jumped off of it and onto a (**2.**) _____. I don't know how he kept his balance! And then, while still riding, someone gave him a (**3.**) _____, and he played the most beautiful song. I would have thought he'd be too out of breath to play anything! The only part I didn't like was when they brought out what they said was a (**4.**) _____. I could tell it was just a (**5.**) _____ with a fake horn strapped to her head. It was silly. I wanted to see more of the clown!

Directions: Spell each new word three times.

1. trampoline   _____   _____   _____
2. mare   _____   _____   _____
3. unicorn   _____   _____   _____
4. unicycle   _____   _____   _____
5. saxophone   _____   _____   _____

Activity: Fill in the blanks with the best new vocabulary word.

1. That jazz band's _____ player really played his instrument well.

2. You must always be careful when jumping up and down on a _____ .

3. The _____ was resting after giving birth to the brown colt.

4. In the fairy tale, a young prince rode in on a white _____ and saved the girl from the evil witch.

5. I don't think I'd be very good at riding a _____ . I think I prefer a bike that has two wheels.

Dig It, Girl!

Directions: Find the meaning of each underlined word in the newspaper article. Put the letter of the answer on the blank line. Use the definitions box to help you.

A. to make a guess based on facts

B. referring to the time before there were written records

C. the part of the skeleton that is the head

D. a wild pig with tusks

E. something made by humans, usually from a much earlier time

LOCAL GIRL MAKES IMPORTANT DISCOVERY

1. _____

2. _____

3. _____

4. _____

5. _____

Erika Ginter, 8, has always liked to dig. But no one ever thought it would make her famous. But that's just what happened when, while digging in her backyard, she found two [1]prehistoric objects. One was the [2]skull of a type of [3]boar that no longer exists. The other—found in the same place—was an [4]artifact that scientists believe was a kind of cup or bowl. It is believed that a hunter had a meal in the very spot that Erika dug up. Scientists [5]estimate that this happened about 25,000 years ago. The objects can be seen in the museum at the local college.

Directions: Spell each new word three times.

1. prehistoric _____ _____ _____

2. skull _____ _____ _____

3. boar _____ _____ _____

4. artifact _____ _____ _____

5. estimate _____ _____ _____

Activity: Match each idea to the best new word. Put the letter of the idea on the line next to the word.

_____ 1. prehistoric

_____ 2. skull

_____ 3. boar

_____ 4. artifact

_____ 5. estimate

A. This protects your brain.

B. This animal wouldn't make a good pet.

C. This happened a very long time ago.

D. This could be your best guess.

E. This might prove that someone else lived here.

Advice for Life

Directions: Read the following short magazine article. Use the mini dictionary to help you fill in the missing words.

> **dissimilar** — not alike
> **identical** — exactly the same
> **bore** — to make a hole
>
> **artist** — someone who shows great skill at something
> **patio** — a concrete outside area attached to a house or other building

PUTTING THE "YOU" IN YOUR HOUSE

Many people think of a house as just the place where they live. But you will like living there more if you make your house really yours. One way to do this is to learn to work on it yourself. Don't just pay someone to put a **(1.)** _____ in—make the plans and pour the cement yourself. Want to build a wooden railing? **(2.)** _____ the holes yourself. However, it takes a real **(3.)** _____ to make all his or her holes **(4.)** _____ . If you don't know what you're doing, your holes will all be **(5.)** _____ —not good if you want your house to be just perfect! Study hard and work hard, and you can make your home your own.

Directions: Spell each new word three times.

1. dissimilar _____ _____ _____
2. identical _____ _____ _____
3. bore _____ _____ _____
4. artist _____ _____ _____
5. patio _____ _____ _____

Activity: Circle the word in each group that does not belong.

1. artist	expert	amateur	master
2. identical	unlike	different	unique
3. bore	punch	poke	fill
4. patio	kitchen	bedroom	bathroom
5. dissimilar	original	unequal	same

Coming Soon

Directions: Find the meaning of each underlined word in the flyer below. Put the letter of the answer on the blank line. Use the definitions box to help you.

> A. to make someone tired of something because it is not fun or interesting
> B. a person's sense of humor
> C. showing a little bit of something before showing the whole thing
> D. liked by a lot of people
> E. the chance that something will happen

DO YOU LIKE TO LAUGH?

1. _____
2. _____
3. _____
4. _____
5. _____

If you do, be sure to be on time when you see a movie at our Cineplex 10 Theater this week. That's because before each movie, there will be a very special [1]preview of the next film starring America's most [2]popular comedy actor. Not only do we promise that it won't [3]bore you, there is a 100% [4]probability that it will tickle your [5]funny bone. See you at the movies!

Directions: Spell each new word three times.

1. preview _____ _____ _____

2. popular _____ _____ _____

3. bore _____ _____ _____

4. probability _____ _____ _____

5. funny bone _____ _____ _____

Activity: Put all of your new words in ABC order. Then, on the line next to each word, use the word in a sentence.

1. _____ _____

2. _____ _____

3. _____ _____

4. _____ _____

5. _____ _____

Setting an Example

Directions: Read the following dialogue. Use the mini dictionary to help you fill in the missing words.

> **appear** — to seem, to look like
>
> **supermarket** — a large store that sells many kinds of food and other things
>
> **takeout** — a type of restaurant that sells ready-to-eat food for you to take home
>
> **displease** — to make unhappy or angry
>
> **neighborhood** — the area near to a person's house

"What are we going to have for dinner, Dad?"

"What do we have here?"

"There's nothing, really. We need to go to the (**1.**) _____."

"Oh, I hate it when your mother is out of town."

"I do, too. Your cooking is terrible."

"I know. Hey, isn't there a new (**2.**) _____ place in the (**3.**) _____?"

"Yeah. It's Japanese food."

"Excellent! Let's go."

"It would (**4.**) _____ Mom if she knew."

"Then it would (**5.**) _____ that we better not tell her, right?"

Directions: Spell each new word three times.

1. appear _____ _____ _____
2. supermarket _____ _____ _____
3. takeout _____ _____ _____
4. displease _____ _____ _____
5. neighborhood _____ _____

Activity: Circle the best answer to each of the following phrases.

1. place to get a loaf of bread   **takeout** or **supermarket**
2. place to get a burger and fries   **takeout** or **neighborhood**
3. place you come home to   **neighborhood** or **appear**
4. something that doesn't make you happy   **appear** or **displease**
5. when you look, this is what you see   **appear** or **displease**

Little Mystery

Directions: Find the meaning of each underlined word in the story. Put the letter of the answer on the blank line. Use the definitions box to help you.

A. a short note after the main part
   of something
B. to make bigger

C. spooky, weird
D. a machine that can make copies of pages
E. happy, thrilled

1. _____

2. _____

3. _____

4. _____

5. _____

Someone had left a magazine on my desk full of short mystery stories. I read a couple, and they were great! It was almost as if this magazine had been written with me in mind, and I wanted to know who had made it. I found the page that listed the writers and where and when it was printed. But then at the bottom I noticed a ¹postscript in the tiniest writing I had ever seen—much too tiny for me to read. I tried using a magnifying glass, but it was no use. Then, I had an idea. I went to the library to use the ²photocopier there. Sure enough, I could ³enlarge any copy I made. I made a copy, then made a copy of the copy, each time making the part I wanted to read bigger. I was ⁴excited when I finally made a copy in which the words were big enough to read. I'll never forget the ⁵eerie feeling I had as I began to read: "Someone had left a magazine on my desk full of short mystery stories. I read a couple, and they were great! It was almost as if . . ."

Directions: Spell each new word three times.

1. postscript   _____   _____   _____

2. photocopier   _____   _____   _____

3. enlarge   _____   _____   _____

4. excited   _____   _____   _____

5. eerie   _____   _____   _____

Activity: Put all of your new words in ABC order. Then, on the line next to each word, use the word in a sentence.

1. _____   _____

2. _____   _____

3. _____   _____

4. _____   _____

5. _____   _____

An American Party

Directions: Read the following invitation. Use the mini dictionary to help you fill in the missing words.

> **futon** — a firm Japanese mattress rolled out and used as a bed
>
> **foreign** — of another place or culture
>
> **condo** — short for "condominium": an apartment that is owned by an individual but is part of a larger building
>
> **ravioli** — a pasta shell stuffed with meat, cheese, and/or vegetable
>
> **kinship** — feeling or being related to

YOU ARE INVITED TO A SURPRISE PARTY FOR SCOTT NUTTEN

We all love Scott, but let's face it—the (**1.**) _____ he feels for anything that's (**2.**) _____ drives us a little crazy sometimes. He'll only sleep on a (**3.**) _____ , he'll only eat foods like sushi and (**4.**) _____ , he'll only play ice hockey and cricket and not football or baseball. Well, for his birthday this year, we're going to have an "All American" party. While he's out, we're going to decorate his (**5.**) _____ in red, white, and blue, and we're going to have American foods like hamburgers and chili. Please RSVP by this weekend with any ideas you may have. See you there!

Directions: Spell each new word three times.

1. futon _____ _____ _____
2. foreign _____ _____ _____
3. condo _____ _____ _____
4. ravioli _____ _____ _____
5. kinship _____ _____ _____

Activity: Circle the word in each group that does not belong.

1. futon	sofa	chair	blanket
2. ravioli	broccoli	celery	cucumber
3. foreign	familiar	strange	unfamiliar
4. condo	hello	limo	mayo
5. kinship	relation	association	disassociation

Too Sloppy for School

Directions: Find the meaning of each underlined word in the memo. Put the letter of the answer on the blank line. Use the definitions box to help you.

> A. the branch of mathematics concerned with points, lines, angles, and shapes
> B. a mistake in typing
> C. agreeing, being the same
> D. a book for learning, usually in school
> E. a straight line passing through the middle of an object from one side to the other

To: Printing Department
From: Cam Gregson, Editor
Re: **mistakes in project**

1. _____
2. _____
3. _____
4. _____
5. _____

It has just come to my attention that the [1]geometry [2]textbook we have just begun printing has at least one [3]typo on every drawing, and we cannot ship it to schools with these kinds of mistakes. Here is an example from page 5: "Find the [4]congruent of the circle below." If you look at the drawing, what the students are supposed to measure is the line running through the middle of the circle—so clearly the word should be "[5]diameter." If we didn't change this, then students might be looking for a circle that is the same size as the one in the drawing—but there are no other circles on the page! So, please stop printing immediately, and we will get you a fixed version of the book as soon as we can.

Directions: Spell each new word three times.

1. geometry _____ _____ _____
2. textbook _____ _____ _____
3. typo _____ _____ _____
4. congruent _____ _____ _____
5. diameter _____ _____ _____

Activity: Circle the best answer to each of the following phrases.

1. distance from one end of a circle to another   **diameter** or **congruent**
2. class where you'd learn about triangles   **geometry** or **textbook**
3. two rectangles that are the same   **typo** or **congruent**
4. where you'd learn about the War of 1812   **textbook** or **geometry**
5. "I have two cats. I want threee someday."   **congruent** or **typo**

Fish Concerns

Directions: Read the following short piece. Use the mini dictionary to help you fill in the missing words.

> **fret** — worry
> **aquarium** — a glass tank in which fish are kept
> **aquatic** — of or having to do with water
>
> **bass** — a common freshwater fish
> **polliwog** — a tadpole

There is a lake by our new house, and some frogs live there. The first day I was there, I saw a (**1.**) _____. It was so small that I was lucky to notice it! I had a plastic bag in my pocket, and I used it to fish the little creature out. I decided right then and there that I would take it home and put it in our (**2.**) _____ to watch it eventually become a frog. Our family loves (**3.**) _____ animals, and we didn't have any because we had just moved.

The next day my dad left before any of us woke up. He had told us he was going to the lake to catch a (**4.**) _____ , his favorite fish. I didn't think anything about it when I left for the day to register for school. But as I was coming home, I began to (**5.**) _____—my tadpole! My dad's fish would eat it! I ran home as fast as I could. When I walked through the door, I smelled something delicious . . . and I realized my dad had caught the fish to eat it, not to keep it as a pet. Whew!

Directions: Spell each new word three times.

1. fret _____ _____ _____
2. bass _____ _____ _____
3. aquarium _____ _____ _____
4. aquatic _____ _____ _____
5. polliwog _____ _____ _____

Activity: Put all of your new words in ABC order. Then, next to each word, write the meaning of the word as it's used on this page.

1. _____ _____
2. _____ _____
3. _____ _____
4. _____ _____
5. _____ _____

Music to My Ears

Directions: Find the meaning of each underlined word in the music review. Put the letter of the answer on the blank line. Use the definitions box to help you.

A. an American type of mostly instrumental music in which the musicians play in response to what each other is doing
B. each of a series of bars or ridges on the fingerboard of a stringed instrument
C. extremely happy
D. an instrument usually having four strings that can play lower notes than a guitar
E. showing off

1. _____

2. _____

3. _____

4. _____

5. _____

The Blue Notes played a set at the Club Music last Saturday that was so good it put the audience in a ¹joyous mood. Club Music is a great place to hear music—it's so small that you can actually feel the low notes of the ²bass vibrating in your body. The Blue Notes play ³jazz as it was meant to be played, each player carefully listening to what the other four are doing. They played many classic pieces by greats such as Miles Davis and John Coltrane, though this reviewer's favorites were the ones by Thelonious Monk. I have only two complaints. One was the guitarist, who seemed to spend too much time in each song keeping his fingers on just one ⁴fret instead of moving them about to create more of a variety in what he played. The other is the drummer. He's great, but sometimes he's too ⁵flashy, which can get in the way of what his bandmates play. Overall, though, this was a great night of music.

Directions: Spell each new word three times.

1. joyous _____ _____ _____
2. bass _____ _____ _____
3. jazz _____ _____ _____
4. fret _____ _____ _____
5. flashy _____ _____ _____

Activity: Put all of your new words in ABC order. Then, next to each word, write the meaning of the word as it's used on this page.

1. _____ _____
2. _____ _____
3. _____ _____
4. _____ _____
5. _____ _____

Everything That Money Can Buy

Directions: Read the following news article. Use the mini dictionary to help you fill in the missing words.

> **royalty** — the members of the family of a king or queen
> **suite** — a set of rooms or other things that belong together
> **caboose** — a car for workmen on a train, usually at the back
> **depot** — a train or bus station
> **heliport** — a place where helicopters take off and land

WORLD'S RICHEST MAN VISITS TOWN

Yesterday, the richest man in the world, Bo Koodinero finally came to our little town. His visit has been planned for the last six months. During that time, he had a (**1.**) _____ built right next to the train station, because he doesn't like to fly in planes or drive in cars. His helicopter landed at noon. After a short look around, he walked straight into the (**2.**) _____ to wait for his private train. While waiting, he was treated like (**3.**) _____ , with workers doing everything he asked—including bringing him a bowl of water so that he could wash his face. After about an hour, his train came in. There were just two cars: the engine and a (**4.**) _____ that had been made into a (**5.**) _____ of rooms for him to use for his two-day trip through the mountains.

Directions: Spell each new word three times.

1. royalty _____ _____ _____
2. suite _____ _____ _____
3. caboose _____ _____ _____
4. depot _____ _____ _____
5. heliport _____ _____ _____

Activity: Fill in the blank in each sentence with the vocabulary word that fits best.

1. After the train's _____ passed by, we were able to cross the train tracks.

2. My uncle landed his helicopter on the _____ located on the roof of the building.

3. We waited at the _____ for the 6:00 train to arrive.

4. I expected to be treated like _____ on my birthday but no one even said a word to me!

5. Our hotel room was dirty so the manager gave us the best _____ in the building. It had two bathrooms!

Better Than the Zoo

Directions: Find the meaning of each underlined word in the short piece. Put the letter of the answer on the blank line. Use the definitions box to help you.

A. happy, cheerful

B. sure-footed and graceful

C. a female deer

D. the male of various animals, including deer and rabbit

E. to play with lots of energy

1. _____
2. _____
3. _____
4. _____
5. _____

I love animals, but many zoos make me unhappy. I hate seeing animals in cages. I like national parks and nature preserves better. The last time I went to one, I was lucky enough to see two deer. I think the ¹buck was trying to get the ²doe to like him. They would ³romp and play for awhile, then rest, then do it some more. I couldn't believe how ⁴nimble they were! Professional athletes can't move like that! And both of them seemed so ⁵jovial with each other! Even though I am just a human, it was easy to see that these two animals were having fun. I've never seen anything like that at a zoo.

Directions: Spell each new word three times.

1. buck   _____   _____   _____

2. doe   _____   _____   _____

3. romp   _____   _____   _____

4. nimble   _____   _____   _____

5. jovial   _____   _____   _____

Activity: An analogy is a comparison between two groups of things. Use your vocabulary words to fill in the analogies below.

1. upset is to sad as _____ is to happy

2. _____ is to play as stroll is to walk

3. graceful is to awkward as _____ is to clumsy

4. woman is to man as _____ is to _____.

Making the Most of Vacation

Directions: Read the following dialog. Use the mini dictionary to help you fill in the missing words.

> **motel** — a small roadside hotel
> **laziness** — slowness, sluggishness, lack of interest in doing anything
> **ski** — to move across snow on long, thin pieces of wood, etc., worn on the feet
> **sunburn** — a reddening of the skin from too much sun
> **envious** — jealous

"Honey, you better get ready to go. We're leaving soon."

"Oh, Mom, I just feel like staying here."

"Don't you want to come to the mountain and (**1.**) _____ with us?"

"No. You guys go without me."

"Are you not feeling well, or is this just pure (**2.**) _____? You've been here in the (**3.**) _____ all day."

"My (**4.**) _____ is hurting a bit."

"It doesn't look too bad. We'll put some extra sunscreen on your face."

"I don't know. I just feel like lying around."

"Okay, but I hope you're not too (**5.**) _____ when we get back and tell you how great it was."

"Alright! You're right. I'll come."

Directions: Spell each new word three times.

1. motel   _____   _____   _____
2. laziness   _____   _____   _____
3. ski   _____   _____   _____
4. sunburn   _____   _____   _____
5. envious   _____   _____   _____

Activity: Match each idea to the best new word. Put the letter of the idea on the line next to the word.

_____	1. motel	A. Phil does nothing all day.
_____	2. laziness	B. Annie wishes she could nothing all day.
_____	3. ski	C. Sanjay stays here when he goes on vacation.
_____	4. sunburn	D. Rudy has this from playing outside all day.
_____	5. envious	E. Miguel does this whenever it snows.

The World's Fair

Directions: Find the meaning of each underlined word in the short piece. Put the letter of the answer on the blank line. Use the definitions box to help you.

> A. a type of train that runs on one rail
> B. a feeling of togetherness
> C. having many uses
> D. amazing and worth talking about
> E. a ride with cars that carry people up and down in a circle

1. _____
2. _____
3. _____
4. _____
5. _____

The World's Fair is a [1]remarkable event. It is usually held in a big city, and it usually lasts for several months. It changes the world around it. For example, a [2]monorail was built for the Seattle World's Fair in 1962, and it's still in use today. And did you know that the first [3]Ferris wheel was built for the World's Fair in Chicago in 1893? People loved riding it so much that you don't need to go to a World's Fair to ride one now! But the World's Fair is a [4]multipurpose event. It's not just for building big things, it's a chance for [5]brotherhood, for people from all over the world to come together in one place and share with each other their ideas and culture.

Directions: Spell each new word three times.

1. remarkable _____ _____ _____
2. monorail _____ _____ _____
3. Ferris wheel _____ _____ _____
4. multipurpose _____ _____ _____
5. brotherhood _____ _____ _____

Activity: Match each idea to the best new word. Put the letter of the idea on the line next to the word.

1. remarkable _____
2. monorail _____
3. Ferris wheel _____
4. multipurpose _____
5. brotherhood _____

A. This is an amusement-park ride.
B. This can do many things.
C. This can get you where from one place to another.
D. With this, everybody gets along together.
E. This is special and different.

Rain Without One Rhyme

Directions: Read the poem. Use the mini dictionary to help you fill in the missing words.

> **twirl** — to spin
> **torrent** — a large flow of anything, such as water
> **umbrella** — a portable device that opens to protect against rain or sun
> **unfurl** — to open and spread out
> **trickle** — a slow flow of drops or a small stream

Who Needs the Sun?

The sky was gray with beautiful clouds
The air was cold and sharp
I buttoned my coat and began to walk
A slow (**1.**) _____ of rain began to fall
I pushed a button on the handle of my (**2.**) _____
And watched it quickly (**3.**) _____
I made it (**4.**) _____
The rain became a (**5.**) _____
The wind tried to blow me down
But I would not go back inside
On such a beautiful day

Directions: Spell each new word three times.

1. twirl _____ _____ _____
2. torrent _____ _____ _____
3. umbrella _____ _____ _____
4. unfurl _____ _____ _____
5. trickle _____ _____ _____

Activity: Fill in the blanks in each sentence with one new word.

1. We were lost, so I had to _____ my map and try to find our location.
2. Out of nowhere, a _____ of rain fell and got us completely soaked.
3. Luckily, I had an_____ to keep some of the rain off of us.
4. Phoebe played around in the rain and did a little _____ like a dancer.
5. We laughed and clapped as the heavy downpour slowed down to a _____.

All Business

Directions: Find the meaning of each underlined word in the business report below. Put the letter of the answer on the blank line. Use the definitions box to help you.

> A. making or earning money
> B. to move from one place to another
> C. to stop
> D. across a continent (such as Africa or Europe)
> E. a telling about something

1. _____
2. _____
3. _____
4. _____
5. _____

"Thank you, ladies and gentlemen. My ¹report will be very brief. I have looked carefully at our company, and it is clear to me that it simply isn't ²profitable for us to keep shipping our products across North America using our ³transcontinental railroad lines. Therefore, we should ⁴discontinue using them. We would be better off using planes and trucks to ⁵transport whatever we sell. That's all I have to say. Any questions?"

Directions: Spell each new word three times.

1. report   _____   _____   _____

2. profitable   _____   _____   _____

3. transcontinental _____   _____   _____

4. discontinue   _____   _____   _____

5. transport   _____   _____   _____

Activity: Match each idea to the best new word. Put the letter of the idea on the line next to the word.

_____ 1. report

_____ 2. profitable

_____ 3. transcontinental

_____ 4. discontinue

_____ 5. transport

A. Our company ships goods from one town to the next.

B. Our company ships goods from New York to California.

C. Our company ships goods that make thousands of dollars.

D. Our company has stopped making these goods.

E. This will explain why our company has stopped making these goods.

Green Snacks

Directions: Read the following recipe. Use the mini dictionary to help you fill in the missing words. (Note: One word will be used twice.)

> **avocado** — a pear-shaped fruit with rough skin and green flesh
> **sandwich** — a meal made of two (or more) slices of bread with other food in between
> **scoop** — 1. (verb) to dig out an amount of something; 2. (noun) the amount dug out
> **mayonnaise** — a thick, creamy, white dressing
> **gingerbread** — a cake made with syrup and flavored with the spice ginger

ST. PATRICK'S DAY SWEET SNACK SURPRISE

- Wait until March 17th.
- Cut one (**1.**) _____ in half and (**2.**) _____ out the flesh.
- Place the flesh in a mixing bowl.
- Add one (**3.**) _____ of (**4.**) _____ .
- Mix together until you have a light green paste.
- Spread this on two pieces of (**5.**) _____ .
- Add salt and pepper.
- Press the pieces together.
- Take a bite of the greenest, gooiest (**6.**) _____ you'll ever have!

Directions: Spell each new word three times.

1. avocado   _____   _____   _____
2. sandwich   _____   _____   _____
3. scoop   _____   _____   _____
4. mayonnaise   _____   _____   _____
5. gingerbread   _____   _____   _____

Activity: Make three new sentences of your own. Follow the directions for each sentence.

1. Write a sentence using the words "sandwich" and "mayonnaise."

   _____

2. Write a sentence using the word "avocado" and the verb "scoop."

   _____

3. Write a sentence using the word "gingerbread" and the noun "scoop."

   _____

To Serve Your Country

Directions: Find the meaning of each underlined word in the below passage from a handbook about being in the Marines. Put the letter of the answer on the blank line. Use the definitions box to help you.

A. to give up or leave

B. braver, more confident

C. a body of troops with special duties

D. to behave

E. very careful and exact

1. _____

2. _____

3. _____

4. _____

5. _____

Members of the Marine ¹Corps must at all times ²comport themselves according to rules. They must be ³methodical in not only the way they act, but even in the way they dress. This helps all Marines feel they are a single group. By feeling this way, they will better be able to act this way and to take orders as one; all doing the same things at the same time when necessary. Marines are also taught never to ⁴desert another Marine when he or she is injured. All of this togetherness helps a Marine to be ⁵bolder in battle than he or she would be on his or her own.

Directions: Spell each new word three times.

1. corps _____ _____ _____

2. comport _____ _____ _____

3. methodical _____ _____ _____

4. desert _____ _____ _____

5. bolder _____ _____ _____

Activity: Put all of your new words in ABC order. Then, next to each word, write the meaning of the word as it's used on this page.

1. _____ _____

2. _____ _____

3. _____ _____

4. _____ _____

5. _____ _____

A Note from Mom

Directions: Find the meaning of each underlined word in the paragraph below. Put the letter of the answer on the blank line. Use the definitions box to help you.

> A. tiny
> B. a small, sweet, orange-colored fruit
> C. a piece of furniture used for storing food, etc.
> D. eating utensils
> E. trash
> F. a sugary, thick liquid

1. _____

2. _____

3. _____

4. _____

5. _____

6. _____

Good morning, my son! I was called in to the hospital to help out. I should be home by late afternoon. Your father and I feel you are old enough to look after yourself during the day.

I know your favorite breakfast is pancakes. In case you're not sure where everything is, you can find the pancake mix in the [1]cupboard. The [2]syrup is in the pantry, but you may use only a [3]minute amount, since too much sugar is bad for you. The [4]cutlery is in the drawer to the right of the refrigerator. Remember to put all of your [5]refuse in the trash compactor. If you want a mid-day snack, no candy! Try a [6]tangerine instead.

Directions: Spell each new word three times.

1. cupboard   _____   _____   _____
2. syrup   _____   _____   _____
3. minute   _____   _____   _____
4. cutlery   _____   _____   _____
5. refuse   _____   _____   _____
6. tangerine   _____   _____   _____

Activity: Your new vocabulary words have been jumbled up. Match each jumbled-up vocabulary word with its definition.

1. try clue   A. tiny
2. engine rat   B. a small, sweet, orange-colored fruit
3. see fur   C. a piece of furniture used for storing food, etc.
4. pry us   D. eating utensils
5. u drab cop   E. trash
6. in mute   F. a sugary, thick liquid

A Good Deed

Directions: Read the following news story. Use the mini dictionary to help you fill in the missing words.

> **gang** — a small group
> **heroic** — like a hero; brave
> **bandit** — a type of criminal who steals
>
> **minute** — 60 seconds
> **refuse** — to say "no" to something
> **hullabaloo** — a lot of noise and activity

GOOD CITIZEN CATCHES THIEF

Al Goodman always thought of himself as ordinary. But Vic Timmerman will tell you a different story. Timmerman, 74, didn't know what had happened when he found himself knocked to the ground. But the people around him did—a (**1.**) _____ had bumped into him, snatched his wallet, and run.

Goodman, 40, was walking down the sidewalk when he saw a man running in his direction. Behind the man he heard a (**2.**) _____ and cries of, "Thief! Thief!" Almost without thinking, he stuck out his foot and tripped the running man. A police car happened to be driving by, and not a (**3.**) _____ later, the thief was in custody. "I don't think of what I did as being (**4.**) _____," Goodman said later, "but I'm just not someone who would ever (**5.**) _____ to help a fellow citizen."

Police later said that the thief was part of a (**6.**) _____ that has been stealing wallets from senior citizens for the last four months.

Directions: Spell each new word three times.

1. gang _____ _____ _____
2. heroic _____ _____ _____
3. bandit _____ _____ _____
4. minute _____ _____ _____
5. refuse _____ _____ _____
6. hullabaloo _____ _____ _____

Activity: Put all of your new words in ABC order. Then, next to each word, write the meaning of the word as it's used on this page.

1. _____ _____
2. _____ _____
3. _____ _____
4. _____ _____
5. _____ _____
6. _____ _____

Diary Full of Homophones

Directions: Find the meaning of each underlined word in the paragraph below. Put the letter of the answer on the blank line. Use the definitions box to help you.

> A. groups of people who work together
> B. headgear used to control a horse
> C. very rough
>
> D. a path or series of directions
> E. having to do with a bride
> F. a trip on a ship

Dear Diary,

1. _____

2. _____

3. _____

4. _____

5. _____

6. _____

Everything to do with my eldest sister's wedding has gone wrong! First, she hated the way her ¹bridal gown turned out. She says the fabric they used to make it is so ²coarse that she could barely stand to wear it. Then, after the ceremony, when they were taking a carriage ride away from the church, first they got off ³course and ended up riding in circles, then the ⁴bridle came off the horse, and it galloped away. After that, her honeymoon ⁵cruise got canceled. Then they bought plane tickets for Hawaii—but all of the airline ⁶crews went on strike, so there was no one to fly the plane! Poor thing!

Directions: Spell each new word three times.

1. bridal _____ _____ _____

2. coarse _____ _____ _____

3. course _____ _____ _____

4. bridle _____ _____ _____

5. cruise _____ _____ _____

6. crews _____ _____ _____

Activity: Fill in the blanks in each sentence with the best new word.

1. The woman's _____ gown was long and white and very beautiful.

2. The gown was made of a soft material, so that it would not be too _____.

3. The married couple took a _____ aboard a ship for their vacation.

4. The ship's work _____ made sure the deck of the boat was dry and clean.

5. The ship went off _____ to avoid a storm and was late arriving.

6. On vacation, the couple learned how to feed a horse and safely put a _____ on its head.

Acronyms

Directions: Read the following piece about this special type of word. Use the mini dictionary to help you fill in the missing words.

> **radar** — "radio detection and ranging"
> **sonar** — "sound navigation and ranging"
> **scuba** — "self-contained underwater breathing apparatus"
>
> **unique** — uncommon
> **laser** — "light amplification by stimulated emission of radiation"
> **quasar** — "quasi-stellar" object

Acronyms are **(1.)** _____ words, because the letters of that word stand for other words. You probably know how to use many acronyms—without even knowing that's what they are! What do you call a very focused beam of light? A **(2.)** _____, of course—and that's an acronym. What do you use when you want to breathe under water? A **(3.)** _____tank—another acronym! Another one, **(4.)** _____, helps you find something in water when you can't see it. Want to find something in the air that's too far away to see? Try this acronym: **(5.)** _____. An acronym that's less common—and much farther away—is **(6.)** _____, which got its name because it was originally thought of as being "part star" because astronomers observed that these looked like stars, except that they were so far away that they had to be much, much more powerful.

Directions: Spell each new word three times.

1. radar _____ _____ _____
2. sonar _____ _____ _____
3. scuba _____ _____ _____
4. unique _____ _____ _____
5. laser _____ _____ _____
6. quasar _____ _____ _____

Activity: Match each idea to the best new word. Put the letter of the idea on the line next to the word.

_____ 1. unique   A. I want to breathe underwater.

_____ 2. laser   B. I need a telescope to see this.

_____ 3. radar   C. This is like no other.

_____ 4. sonar   D. This helps boats find their way.

_____ 5. scuba   E. Planes can be detected by this.

_____ 6. quasar   F. Doctors use these to perform surgery.

Liven Up Your Writing

Directions: Find the meaning of each underlined word in the paragraph below. Put the letter of the answer on the blank line. Use the definitions box to help you.

A. giving human traits to something that is non-human
B. a word that is an imitation of a sound
C. a short, loud, unpleasant animal call
D. to close (with a zipper)
E. a book containing words and their meanings
F. a sequence of words with the same beginning sound

1. _____
2. _____
3. _____
4. _____
5. _____
6. _____

There are many ways to make your writing jump off the page. I just used one of them—[1]personification. People can jump—but writing can't! And there are many more methods I may use to make my material marvelous—like that: [2]alliteration. Both of these are long words. If you see them again but don't remember what they mean, you can look them up in a [3]dictionary. You can find shorter words, too. "He closed his jacket with a [4]zip. A bird made a [5]squawk as it flew overhead." If you look these up, you will see that they are examples of [6]onomatopoeia.

Directions: Spell each new word three times.

1. personification _____   _____   _____

2. alliteration _____   _____   _____

3. dictionary _____   _____   _____

4. zip _____   _____   _____

5. squawk _____   _____   _____

6. onomatopoeia _____   _____   _____

Activity: Draw a line to match each idea to the best new word.

1. The angry sea rages in the night.
2. There was a "Thwack!" each time he hit the ball.
3. I opened my backpack quickly, and it made this sound.
4. Lazy Larry lay on the lawn.
5. How do I spell "onomatopoeia"?
6. Is that a crow making that annoying sound?

A. personification
B. alliteration
C. dictionary
D. zip
E. squawk
F. onomatopoeia

Some Poetry Basics

Directions: Read the following piece about elements of poetry. Use the mini dictionary to help you fill in the missing words.

> **simile** — a comparison between two things using *like* or *as*
> **rhyme** — words with the same ending sound (ex.: *line* and *fine*)
> **couplet** — a pair of lines in a poem
> **meter** — the rhythm of a line of writing
> **haiku** — a short form of poetry originating in Japan
> **sonnet** — a slightly longer form of poetry with a special meter

Not all poems (**1.**) _____. One example is (**2.**) _____, which usually has three lines of five, seven, and five syllables and is about nature. A different sort of poem is the (**3.**) _____, which is 14 lines, has a special (**4.**) _____ (rhythm), and almost always ends in a pair of lines that is called a rhyming (**5.**) _____. Both of these poems may use a (**6.**) _____ (which is a type of metaphor) to compare two things. This example is by William Shakespeare: "My mistress' eyes are nothing like the sun."

Directions: Spell each new word three times.

1. simile _____ _____ _____

2. rhyme _____ _____ _____

3. couplet _____ _____ _____

4. meter _____ _____ _____

5. haiku _____ _____ _____

6. sonnet _____ _____ _____

Activity: Use your new words to write three sentences. Follow the directions given.

1. Write a sentence that includes a simile.

_____

2. Write a sentence that includes two words that rhyme with "rhyme."

_____

3. Write a rhyming couplet.

_____

Early Fireworks

Directions: Find the meaning of each underlined word in the paragraph below. Put the letter of the answer on the blank line. Use the definitions box to help you.

A. a two-piece bathing suit for girls

B. a time of celebration, often including time off from work or school

C. outdoor cooking of food on a grill

D. light shining off or out of something

E. silly

F. to let something happen

1. _____

2. _____

3. _____

4. _____

5. _____

6. _____

All of our relatives were at our house for the Fourth of July ¹holiday for a ²barbecue. I was falling asleep in my chair as I watched the sunlight ³glimmer off the surface of the swimming pool, when I heard my mother and sister arguing. My mother would not ⁴allow my sister to go outside in her new ⁵bikini because it was too small. They were actually yelling at each other over this! I thought the whole thing was ⁶ridiculous. I didn't care who won the argument—I just wanted it to be over so that I could fall asleep!

Directions: Spell each new word three times.

1. holiday _____ _____ _____

2. barbecue _____ _____ _____

3. glimmer _____ _____ _____

4. allow _____ _____ _____

5. bikini _____ _____ _____

6. ridiculous _____ _____ _____

Activity: Fill in the blanks in each sentence with the best new word.

1. My older brother lost a bet and had to walk around at the beach in a _____ for one hour. He looked _____!

2. My sister said that Valentine's Day is her favorite _____. We were all practically blinded by the _____ from the diamond ring her boyfriend gave her last year.

3. Because of the high winds, it's a fire hazard to _____ at the campgrounds this weekend. The fire department has said that they won't _____ it under any circumstances.

Today's News

Directions: Find the meaning of each underlined word in the newspaper headlines. Put the letter of the answer on the blank line. Use the definitions box to help you.

> A. assign, place (in a job)
> B. trap, catch
> C. saying "no" to something (usually by a president)
> D. unite, blend together
> E. writing for a newspaper or magazine
> F. a piece of glass or plastic that protects a driver from the wind, debris, etc.

_____ **1. President Uses <u>Veto</u> to Stop New Law**

_____ **2. Company to Install Safer <u>Windshield</u> on All New Cars**

_____ **3. News Writer to Win <u>Journalism</u> Award For Article**

_____ **4. Team Owner to <u>Appoint</u> New Coach by Friday**

_____ **5. Two Software Companies Agree to <u>Merge</u> Next Year**

_____ **6. Police <u>Snare</u> Bank Robber After Car Chase**

Directions: Spell each new word three times.

1. veto`   _____   _____   _____

2. windshield   _____   _____   _____

3. journalism   _____   _____   _____

4. appoint   _____   _____   _____

5. merge   _____   _____   _____

6. snare   _____   _____   _____

Activity: Cross out the word(s) in each group that does not belong.

1. snare	lose	drop	release
2. merge	break apart	join	come together
3. journalism	poetry	screenwriting	acting
4. windshield	helmet	seatbelt	car stereo
5. appoint	hire	nominate	dismiss
6. disagree	reject	approve	veto

Tips on Being a Hard Worker

Directions: Find the meaning of each underlined word in the paragraph below. Put the letter of the answer on the blank line. Use the definitions box to help you.

A. normal, regular
B. a mistake or mix-up
C. believing that things will work out well

D. great, excellent
E. someone who tries to make something perfect
F. reasonable, practical, realistic

1. _____
2. _____
3. _____
4. _____
5. _____
6. _____

Trying to be a [1]perfectionist can be a good thing, as the extra effort you put in can be the difference between doing an [2]ordinary job and an [3]outstanding one. However, you should be [4]sensible about it. To try to do something perfectly takes some [5]optimism, because you can always run into some sort of [6]snafu. Remember, hard work is good—but we all make mistakes sometimes! All you can ask of yourself is that you try your best.

Directions: Spell each new word three times.

1. perfectionist _____ _____ _____

2. ordinary _____ _____ _____

3. outstanding _____ _____ _____

4. sensible _____ _____ _____

5. optimism _____ _____ _____

6. snafu _____ _____ _____

Activity: Decide if the following pairs are synonyms or antonyms. Write **S** (*for synonym*) or **A** (for *antonym*) in each blank.

1. sensible   practical   _____

2. ordinary   average   _____

3. optimism   pessimism   _____

4. snafu   error   _____

5. perfectionist   lazy person   _____

6. outstanding   unremarkable   _____

Disaster!

Directions: Read the following piece about some dangers of the natural world. Use the mini dictionary to help you fill in the missing words.

> **volcano** — a mountain or hill through which lava may force its way out of the earth
>
> **earthquake** — a shaking of the earth caused by the movement on or below the surface
>
> **cyclone** — a very large circular storm that forms at sea
>
> **whirlpool** — a funnel-shaped, spinning area of water
>
> **underground** — beneath the surface of the earth
>
> **dormant** —not active; sleeping

Nature is full of beauty—but also of danger! For example, imagine you are looking at a peaceful mountain. Suddenly, you feel a shaking. Something is happening **(1.)**_____. Hot liquid rock is pushing its way to the surface, causing an **(2.)** _____. It turns out your wonderful mountain is actually a **(3.)** _____. If it had been **(4.)** _____, you'd be okay—but it's active, and about to erupt!

Maybe you prefer the water to the land—the calm, cool blue and green of the sea. But in the distance you see a giant wall of clouds. It's miles and miles across! That's no ordinary rainstorm—it's a **(5.)** _____! Luckily, it's not coming towards you. But wait! Your boat is starting to be pulled in tighter and tighter circles! The water is trying to suck you under! You're caught in a **(6.)** _____!

Fortunately, although these dangers are real, they are pretty rare, and by knowing about them, you can take steps to avoid them.

Directions: Spell each new word three times.

1. volcano _____ _____ _____
2. earthquake _____ _____ _____
3. cyclone _____ _____ _____
4. whirlpool _____ _____ _____
5. underground _____ _____ _____
6. dormant _____ _____ _____

Activity: On a separate piece of paper, put your new words in ABC order. Then, next to each word, write the meaning.

Too Much to Ask?

Directions: Find the meaning of each underlined word in the classified ad below. Put the letter of the answer on the blank line. Use the definitions box to help you.

> A. a car for hire by the minute to take people from one place to another
> B. a liquid men put on in small amounts to make them smell good
> C. an outfit worn by men at certain special events
> D. not doing what you know you should do
> E. a person who fixes vehicles
> F. a dial that tells how fast a vehicle is going

1. _____
2. _____
3. _____
4. _____
5. _____
6. _____

Wanted: [1]Taxi Driver

Our company is not like any other. First, you must be a [2]mechanic, as we don't have anyone else to fix our cabs. Second, you must be able to read Roman numerals, because the [3]speedometer on your cab will have these instead of the normal Arabic numerals. Third, you must always wear [4]cologne if you're a man or perfume if you're a woman. Fourth, you must own a [5]tuxedo—whether you're a man or a woman—because we want all of our drivers to dress the same way. Lastly, of course, you must not be [6]irresponsible, because we want to offer only the best service. If you think you can live up to our needs, please call (562) 555-2828.

Directions: Spell each new word three times.

1. taxi _____ _____ _____
2. mechanic _____ _____ _____
3. speedometer _____ _____ _____
4. cologne _____ _____ _____
5. tuxedo _____ _____ _____
6. irresponsible _____ _____ _____

Activity: Make three new sentences of your own. Follow the directions for each sentence.

1. Write a sentence using the words "cologne" and "tuxedo." _____

_____

2. Write a sentence using the words "mechanic" and "speedometer."_____

_____

3. Write a sentence using the words "taxi" and "irresponsible." _____

_____

Travel Guide

Directions: Read the following section of a piece about a trip that might be fun to take. Use the mini dictionary to help you fill in the missing words.

> **gorge** — a narrow opening between hills, often with a river at the bottom of it
> **peninsula** — a patch of land that juts out into the water
> **oasis** — an area in the desert that has water and plant life
> **valley** — a low-lying stretch of land surrounded by hills or mountains
> **plateau** — a high, flat area of land
> **vineyard** — an area with vines used for growing grapes for winemaking

For the first stage of your trip, our helicopter will fly you to a beautiful
(**1.**) _____ in the middle of the desert, where you will spend the night
in a tent. In the morning, the helicopter will pick you up. After a flight of about
90 minutes, you will be dropped off on the highest (**2.**) _____ in
the area, where you will have a breathtaking view of a (**3.**) _____, in
the middle of which is a (**4.**) _____ that produces more wine than any
other in the country. Then you will be flown to a (**5.**) _____ that is so
small that in some places you can see the ocean on three sides of you. Before
you get there, though, you will fly over the country's deepest (**6.**) _____,
which has a white-water river running through it.

Directions: Spell each new word three times.

1. gorge _____ _____ _____
2. peninsula _____ _____ _____
3. oasis _____ _____ _____
4. valley _____ _____ _____
5. plateau _____ _____ _____
6. vineyard _____ _____ _____

Activity: Put your new words in ABC order. Then, next to each word, write the meaning.

1. _____ _____
2. _____ _____
3. _____ _____
4. _____ _____
5. _____ _____
6. _____ _____

A Strange Recipe

Directions: Find the meaning of each underlined word in the recipe below. Put the letter of the answer on the blank line. Use the definitions box to help you.

> A. very tasty, delicious
> B. a room or large cupboard for storing food
> C. a smoked sausage sold ready to eat
> D. a small, sweet melon with orange flesh
> E. a sauce made of tomatoes and used as a topping
> F. a sweet and sharp-tasting seed pod eaten as a vegetable

New-Fangled, No-Cook Pizza

1. _____
2. _____
3. _____
4. _____
5. _____
6. _____

Spread out 10 slices of [1]bologna in a circle on a cooking sheet so that they completely overlap. Pour [2]ketchup over the entire circle, then spread it out evenly. Cover tightly in plastic wrap and store in a [3]larder overnight. In the morning, what you have prepared should be dried out. Spoon the flesh out of a [4]cantaloupe, and chop up about an equal amount of [5]okra. Mix in a bowl, then distribute the mixture over the "crust" on the cooking sheet. Now you are ready to enjoy a [6]succulent treat!

Directions: Spell each new word three times.

1. bologna _____ _____ _____

2. ketchup _____ _____ _____

3. larder _____ _____ _____

4. cantaloupe _____ _____ _____

5. okra _____ _____ _____

6. succulent _____ _____ _____

Activity: Draw a line to match each new word with its description.

1. bologna   a vegetable

2. ketchup   a fruit

3. larder   a meat

4. cantaloupe   a taste

5. okra   a sauce

6. succulent   a storage area

Name That Abbreviation

Directions: Use the following clues to fill in the correct abbreviation. Use the mini dictionary to help you fill in the missing words.

> **coed** — short for "co-educational": having both males and females
>
> **limo** — short for "limousine": a nice, usually long car hired to drive people somewhere
>
> **ref** — short for "referee": a person who makes sure the rules are followed in a game
>
> **mic** — short for "microphone": a piece of equipment used to take in sound (for recording or to make it louder)
>
> **grad** — short for "graduate": a student who has completed a course of study (such as middle school)
>
> **fan** — short for "fanatic": someone who likes something very much

After completing 12th grade, I was a high-school (**1.**) _____. For a graduation present, my parents bought me tickets to a San Francisco 49ers game, because they know I am a big (**2.**) _____ of the team. They also hired a (**3.**) _____ to take me to the stadium. To start the game, the (**4.**) _____ did a coin toss to see which team would get the ball first. However, his (**5.**) _____ wasn't working, so we couldn't hear who won. Other than that, the game was great. When I go away to college, I will be living in a (**6.**) _____ dorm—and I'll bet the boys will be impressed that one of their girl housemates loves pro football!

Directions: Spell each new word three times.

1. coed _____ _____ _____
2. limo _____ _____ _____
3. ref _____ _____ _____
4. mic _____ _____ _____
5. grad _____ _____ _____
6. fan _____ _____ _____

Activity: Fill in the blanks in each sentence with the best new word.

1. That _____ is the longest car I've ever seen!
2. I plan on going to Europe during the summer after I become a college _____.
3. I was one of only three boys in my _____ cooking class.
4. I'm not a _____ of the Yankees—I'd rather root for just about any other team.
5. That _____ needs glasses! He's always making the wrong calls.
6. My little sister thought it was very funny when the announcer accidentally dropped his _____.

Obvious Directions

Directions: Find the meaning of each underlined word in the driving directions. Put the letter of the answer on the blank line. Use the definitions box to help you.

> A. 1,000 meters (0.61 miles)
> B. a control that is pushed by the foot
> C. a place where two (or more) streets cross each other
>
> D. thoughtful
> E. against the law
> F. a person who is walking

1. _____
2. _____
3. _____
4. _____
5. _____
6. _____

Back your car out of your driveway. Once you're in the street, push the gas [1]pedal to drive forward. Turn right at the end of your street onto Main Street. After 1 [2]kilometer, you will come to an [3]intersection. If the light is red, stop. If you see a [4]pedestrian, do not run him or her over. That would be [5]illegal. It is also [6]considerate not to hit people with your car. When the light is green and the way is clear, go forward. The supermarket will be on your right.

Directions: Spell each new word three times.

1. pedal _____ _____ _____
2. kilometer _____ _____ _____
3. intersection _____ _____ _____
4. pedestrian _____ _____ _____
5. illegal _____ _____ _____
6. considerate _____ _____ _____

Activity: Put your new words in ABC order. Then, next to each word, write the meaning.

1. _____ _____
2. _____ _____
3. _____ _____
4. _____ _____
5. _____ _____
6. _____ _____

Air Tour

Directions: Use the following clues to fill in the correct abbreviation. Use the mini dictionary to help you fill in the missing words.

> **tributary** — a river or stream flowing into a larger river or lake
> **hydroelectric** — electricity generated by the movement of water
> **hydroplane** — an airplane that is equipped to land on water
> **strait** — a narrow passage of water connecting two large bodies of water
> **isthmus** — a narrow piece of land connecting two large bodies of land
> **delta** — a triangle of land built at the mouth of a river by the flowing water

A bus took us to the (**1.**) _____ between the two big islands, where a boat was waiting for us. I'd never taken a boat ride to get into the air, but that's exactly what we did: it took us out to a (**2.**) _____ just sitting there floating! After we climbed into the air, first I saw two of the smaller islands connected by a land bridge, which the pilot told us is called an (**3.**) _____. Before long we were flying over the mainland. We started at the south, where I could see the (**4.**) _____ of a big river. We followed the river north. At one point I saw a big (**5.**) _____ dam, which the pilot said provided power for a whole city! As we continued north, I saw one (**6.**) _____ flowing into the river, then another, then a third. I was sorry when the plane circled back to where we'd started for a landing. It was a great flight!

Directions: Spell each new word three times.

1. tributary _____ _____ _____
2. hydroelectric _____ _____ _____
3. hydroplane _____ _____ _____
4. strait _____ _____ _____
5. isthmus _____ _____ _____
6. delta _____ _____ _____

Activity: Match each idea to the correct word. Place the letter of the answer in the blank.

1. water on both sides   A. tributary
2. travels in the air, lands in the water   B. hydroelectric
3. makes power from water   C. hydroplane
4. land on both sides   D. strait
5. water on three sides   E. isthmus
6. flows into a river   F. delta

One-of-a-Kind Garage Sale

Directions: Find the meaning of each underlined word in the ad for a garage sale. Put the letter of the answer on the blank line. Use the definitions box to help you.

> A. a device used to measure temperature
> B. a stroller or "baby buggy"
> C. hypnotized, amazed
>
> D. a type of plant with many-colored flowers
> E. a Japanese type of long, loose robe
> F. a random variety or mish-mash

GARAGE SALE SUNDAY—NOT YOUR USUAL ¹<u>HODGEPODGE</u>

1. _____
2. _____
3. _____
4. _____
5. _____
6. _____

Come to 800 Ocean Boulevard starting at 9 A.M., and you will find some great deals on items so rare that they will leave you ²<u>spellbound</u>! Have you ever taken your temperature with a diamond ³<u>thermometer</u>? We have two for sale! Need a ⁴<u>kimono</u> for your pet gorilla? We've got one that should fit perfectly. Do you have a friend who likes plants but doesn't know how to keep them alive? Stop by Sunday and buy him or her a ⁵<u>dahlia</u> that is easy to take care of! Too tired to take your baby for a stroll? Pick up the motorized ⁶<u>pram</u> we have for sale. If you're looking for some one-of-a-kind items, make sure you're here Sunday!

Directions: Spell each new word three times.

1. hodgepodge _____ _____ _____
2. spellbound _____ _____ _____
3. thermometer _____ _____ _____
4. kimono _____ _____ _____
5. dahlia _____ _____ _____
6. pram _____ _____ _____

Activity: Cross out the word in each group that does not belong.

1. stroller	pram	carriage	unicycle
2. tulip	sycamore	rose	dahlia
3. tuxedo	bathrobe	kimono	helmet
4. spellbound	awed	uninterested	amazed
5. mixture	ingredient	jumble	hodgepodge
6. igloo	thermometer	yardstick	measuring cup

The Winner

Directions: Find the meaning of each underlined word in the story. Use the mini dictionary to help you fill in the missing words.

> **daunting** — intimidating, scary
> **flabbergasted** — totally surprised, shocked
> **fiddlesticks** — an expression of doubt or disbelief; "nonsense!"
> **magazine** — a publication with stories and pictures
> **oxygen** — an element that animals (including humans) breathe
> **lollygag** — to fail to get around to doing something; dilly-dally

When I entered the contest for the best idea for improving the city, I never dreamed I'd win—so when I heard that I did, I was (**1.**) _____! My mother didn't believe me when I told her. " (**2.**) _____!" she said. It wasn't until a writer from a (**3.**) _____ called to interview me that Mom knew it was true. At that point, she got so excited that she thought she would faint. "I can't breathe," she said. "I need some (**4.**) _____!" Suddenly, I felt like I would faint, too—but for a different reason. I'd won the contest for my idea, but now I had to make it a reality. This was a (**5.**)_____ task, as it involved a lot of work. I figured I'd better not (**6.**) _____, and so I went straight up to my room to start working right away.

Directions: Spell each new word three times.

1. daunting _____ _____ _____
2. flabbergasted_____ _____ _____
3. fiddlesticks _____ _____ _____
4. magazine _____ _____ _____
5. oxygen _____ _____ _____
6. lollygag _____ _____ _____

Activity: Cross out the word in each group that does not belong.

1. oxygen	helium	hydrogen	telephone
2. shocked	amazed	bored	flabbergasted
3. daunting	scary	troubling	simple
4. radio	book	magazine	dictionary
5. lollygag	hustle	hurry	rush
6. "Fiddlesticks!"	"No way!"	"Boo!"	"That's crazy!"

The Animal World

Directions: Find the meaning of each underlined word in the passage. Put the letter of the answer on the blank line. Use the definitions box to help you.

> A. a medium-sized antelope that can jump very high
> B. a small type of fish
> C. a flock of geese
> D. a large, meat-eating type of lizard that spends much of its time in water
> E. the largest type of spider
> F. a shoal, or group, of fish

1. _____
2. _____
3. _____
4. _____
5. _____
6. _____

Some animals that look dangerous really are. An [1]alligator, for example, will even attack people if they wander into its territory. But some animals just look scary. You might be terrified if you see a [2]tarantula crawling towards you, but really you would be in no danger at all. Some animals have special names for their groups. Most people think of cans when they think of a group of [3]sardines, but they swim in a [4]school. Geese, meanwhile, fly in a [5]gaggle. Then there are some animals that have the same name whether you mean one of them or many, such as sheep and [6]impala.

Directions: Spell each new word three times.

1. alligator   _____   _____   _____
2. tarantula   _____   _____   _____
3. sardines   _____   _____   _____
4. school   _____   _____   _____
5. gaggle   _____   _____   _____
6. impala   _____   _____   _____

Activity: Use your new vocabulary words to fill in the blanks in these sentences.

1. My _____ was born with only seven legs. It doesn't seem to bother him!
2. The _____ of salmon swam upstream together.
3. I buy a whole bucket of _____ to use as bait when I go fishing.
4. On TV, they showed an _____ running across a field. Those things are fast!
5. I still have a headache from hearing a whole _____ of geese honking outside my door the other night.
6. I never want to get too close to an _____. Those things have huge mouths!

No, Thanks!

Directions: Find the meaning of each underlined word in the piece below. Put the letter of the answer on the blank line. Use the definitions box to help you.

> A. money or things somebody has taken or received
> B. to disagree or have a problem with
> C. to give
>
> D. a thing
> E. a gift
> F. a guitar-like instrument with a long neck and a pear-shaped body

1. _____

2. _____

3. _____

4. _____

5. _____

6. _____

Who knew my 12th birthday would [1]present me with such a problem? "Happy birthday," my friend Paul said when I answered the door that day. "I'd like to give you this [2]present," he said and gave me an [3]object that looked sort of like a guitar.

"Wow, what is that?" I asked.

"It's a [4]lute." It seemed like a strange thing to give me, since I didn't play any instruments, but I liked it.

Later that night, I showed it to my dad, who is a teacher at the high school. He was very interested in it. "Where did you get this?" he asked. I told him. "Well, this was stolen from my school! See, it has the school's initials on the back."

The next day I went to my friend's house. "I don't want your stolen [5]loot!" I said. "And I [6]object to anyone who steals! You have to return this."

With that, I turned around and walked home. I was sad, but I felt it was important to do the right thing.

Directions: Spell each new word three times.

1. present _____ _____ _____

2. present _____ _____ _____

3. object _____ _____ _____

4. object _____ _____ _____

5. lute _____ _____ _____

6. loot _____ _____ _____

Activity: Write three sentences using your new words. In the sentences, use…

1. "present" as a noun (PREZ•ent) and "object" as a verb (ob•JECT). _____

2. "present" as a verb (pre•ZENT) and the noun "loot."

_____

3. "object" as a noun (OB•ject) and the noun "lute."

_____

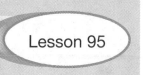

World War II

Directions: Read the following piece about American military action in Germany during the middle of the 20th century. Use the mini dictionary to help you fill in the missing words.

> **substantial** — major, significant
> **generally** — most of the time; in most cases
> **paratroops** — military troops who parachute into battle
>
> **permanent** — forever
> **rash** — acting without thinking; hasty without a planned end
> **declaration** — a statement (often an official one)

War is a very serious and terrible thing. (**1.**) _____, a country will not be (**2.**) _____ about fighting another country. This is what happened with the United States during World War II. Nazi Germany had been fighting and taking over its neighboring countries for several years before 1941, when the U.S. finally made a (**3.**) _____ of war against Germany. Within a couple of years, the U.S. had a very (**4.**) _____ military force fighting Germany. One of the major parts of this force was the (**5.**) _____, who were able to be dropped into Germany behind the lines of troops trying to keep the Americans out of the country. When the war ended, the U.S. had a (**6.**) _____ force in the German capital of Berlin.

Directions: Spell each new word three times.

1. substantial _____ _____ _____

2. generally _____ _____ _____

3. paratroops _____ _____ _____

4. permanent _____ _____ _____

5. rash _____ _____ _____

6. declaration _____ _____ _____

Activity: Make three new sentences of your own. Use two new words in each sentence.

1. _____

2. _____

3. _____

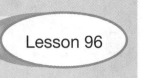

Fear of the Dentist

Directions: Find the meaning of each underlined word in the piece below. Put the letter of the answer on the blank line. Use the definitions box to help you.

> A. without caring about or taking notice of
> B. totally without good reason
> C. a doctor whose area of knowledge is teeth
>
> D. reasonable
> E. very bad or harsh
> F. very many

1. _____
2. _____
3. _____
4. _____
5. _____
6. _____

¹Numerous people are afraid of the ²dentist, but this is an ³irrational fear. Sure, the pain of teeth problems can be ⁴brutal. However, people can avoid most problems with their teeth if they just take care of them. What is ⁵valid is to be afraid of not brushing and flossing enough and of eating foods that hurt their teeth—because that's what causes the problems (and the discomfort and pain that can go with them). If you are not ⁶heedless of the things that can hurt your teeth, having them checked twice a year will almost always be no big deal.

Directions: Spell each new word three times.

1. numerous   _____   _____   _____
2. dentist   _____   _____   _____
3. irrational   _____   _____   _____
4. brutal   _____   _____   _____
5. valid   _____   _____   _____
6. heedless   _____   _____   _____

Activity: Match each idea to the correct word. Place the letter of the answer in the blank.

_____   1. drills and fills cavities   A. numerous

_____   2. without caution   B. dentist

_____   3. a lot   C. irrational

_____   4. makes sense   D. brutal

_____   5. doesn't make sense   E. valid

_____   6. very rough   F. heedless

A Christmas Surprise

Directions: Read the paragraph below. Use the mini dictionary to help you fill in the missing words.

bewildered — totally confused or shocked
frisky — energetic and playful
pajamas — clothing worn for sleeping
blissful — completely happy
sluggish — slow and without energy
compliment — to say something nice about

The best present I ever got was on Christmas Day when I was six years old. Christmas Eve had been wonderful. My parents had gotten me such great gifts that I was too happy to get to sleep until very late, and so in the morning I felt very (**1.**) _____. I got out of bed and walked downstairs in my (**2.**) _____. I was so tired that somehow I completely forgot that Santa Claus had come. There was a little bit of candy in my stocking, and that was all. But that was okay—I had plenty of things. However, when I sat down for breakfast, my mom said, "Santa left you one more present. It's in the living room." When I looked in there, I saw a big box—and it was shaking! I was (**3.**) _____. I opened it, and inside was the most (**4.**) _____ little dog I had ever seen! I loved him right away! I told myself that if I ever met Santa, I would have to (**5.**) _____ him on his good taste. That was the most (**6.**) _____ Christmas ever!

Directions: Spell each new word three times.

1. bewildered   _____   _____   _____
2. frisky   _____   _____   _____
3. pajamas   _____   _____   _____
4. blissful   _____   _____   _____
5. sluggish   _____   _____   _____
6. compliment   _____   _____   _____

Activity: Decide if the following pairs are synonyms or antonyms. Write **S** (for *synonym*) or **A** (for *antonym*) in each blank.

1. compliment   insult   _____
2. blissful   overjoyed   _____
3. pajamas   sleepwear   _____
4. sluggish   energetic   _____
5. frisky   sleepy   _____
6. bewildered   puzzled   _____

A Letter from Camp

Directions: Find the meaning of each underlined word in the letter below. Put the letter of the answer on the blank line. Use the definitions box to help you.

A. not steady	D. energy
B. shaking, trembling	E. dangerous
C. deserving pity; sad	F. an animal that walks on two legs

1. _____

2. _____

3. _____

4. _____

5. _____

6. _____

Dear Mom and Dad,

I got a real scare today. A few of us were walking in the forest, when we saw a tall, hairy ¹biped not far off our path. "Oh wow," Eric whispered, "I think that's Bigfoot!" We stood perfectly still, feeling we were in a ²hazardous situation. I was ³quivering all over and my legs were ⁴unstable, like all of the ⁵vigor had been taken out of them. I must've looked ⁶pathetic. Just then, "Bigfoot" took off his "head"—and it was Mr. Moore, the head counselor. "April Fools!" he laughed. We'd totally forgotten what day it was. I'm not sure I like jokes like this. But I'm having a great time here. See you in two weeks.

Love,

Greg

Directions: Spell each new word three times.

1. biped _____   _____   _____
2. hazardous _____   _____   _____
3. quivering _____   _____   _____
4. unstable _____   _____   _____
5. vigor _____   _____   _____
6. pathetic _____   _____   _____

Activity: Decide if the following pairs are synonyms or antonyms. Write **S** (for *synonym*) or **A** (for *antonym*) in each blank.

1. hazardous   safe   _____
2. vigor   tiredness   _____
3. pathetic   pitiful   _____
4. unstable   steady   _____
5. quivering   shaking   _____
6. biped   two-footed creature _____

A Pretend Election

Directions: Read the following news story about an election. Use the mini dictionary to help you fill in the missing words.

> **veep** — abbreviation of "vice-president"
> **dictator** — a leader with complete power
> **predict** — to guess, usually based on studying information
> **declare** — to say
> **reform** — to improve by removing problems
> **biannual** — twice a year

ELECTION BLOG

In the next few days, we expect Reginald Mifflestaff to once again (**1.**) _____ that he is running for president of our science club for the 8th time. Since our elections are (**2.**) _____, that means he has been in power for 4 years. It's easy to (**3.**) _____ who will win the election, because, just like with the last seven, Mifflestaff will be the only person running! Everyone knows that that he is a (**4.**) _____ and not a president. This can be seen even in many things that he says, such as his answer as to why he doesn't have a vice-president. "I don't need a (**5.**) _____," he said. "I can do it all myself." Somebody else needs to step forward and take charge of this organization. Our club needs (**6.**) _____, and it starts at the top!

Directions: Spell each new word three times.

1. veep	_____	_____	_____
2. dictator	_____	_____	_____
3. predict	_____	_____	_____
4. declare	_____	_____	_____
5. reform	_____	_____	_____
6. biannual	_____	_____	_____

Activity: Draw a line to match each idea with the best new word.

1. "We'll do this every six months."   A. veep
2. "I'm the boss! You do what I tell you to do."   B. dictator
3. "Let's change how we do things."   C. predict
4. "I think the Colts will win next year's Super Bowl."   D. declare
5. "I am second in command."   E. reform
6. "I am one of the best dressers in the 4th grade."   F. biannual

Telephone Ad for Help

Directions: Find the meaning of each underlined word in the ad below. Put the letter of the answer on the blank line. Use the definitions box to help you.

A. to write by having someone else write down what you say
B. pages of writing that are a single unpublished work
C. a very great work
D. unable to read or write
E. a group of people working together under one name and for money
F. worth thinking about or giving attention to

1. _____
2. _____
3. _____
4. _____
5. _____
6. _____

I am ¹illiterate, but I had an idea for a book. I went to a publishing ²company to see if they would want to help me. They thought my idea was ³interesting, but they said they needed to see the finished ⁴manuscript before deciding whether to publish it. I am now looking for someone to whom I can ⁵dictate my thoughts to. If this sounds good to you and you can type as fast as I am talking, please leave a message after the beep. Together we may create a ⁶masterpiece!

Directions: Spell each new word three times.

1. illiterate _____ _____ _____
2. company _____ _____ _____
3. interesting _____ _____ _____
4. manuscript _____ _____ _____
5. dictate _____ _____ _____
6. masterpiece _____ _____ _____

Activity: Circle the best answer to each of the following phrases.

1. a fascinating book about science **interesting** or **illiterate**
2. speaking while someone else writes what you are saying **dictate** or **company**
3. an incredible work of art **illiterate** or **masterpiece**
4. a place of business **interesting** or **company**
5. a person who hasn't learned how to read yet **manuscript** or **illiterate**
6. an incomplete book about people who work together **company** or **manuscript**

Double Riddles

Directions: Solve each of the following riddles by using two of the words from the mini dictionary.

> **flat** — level
> **recreation** — something that is made again
> **flare** — a fire signal used to get attention
> **recreation** — play, fun
> **flair** — style
> **flat** — a type of apartment

This is enjoying doing something unoriginal.

Answer: (**1.**) _____ (**2.**) _____

Someone might say you have this if your outfit has neat-looking flames.

Answer: (**3.**) _____ (**4.**) _____

A ball could live here without rolling one way or the other.

Answer: (**5.**) _____ (**6.**) _____

Directions: Spell each new word three times.

1. flat   _____ _____ _____

2. recreation _____ _____ _____

3. flare   _____ _____ _____

4. recreation _____ _____ _____

5. flair   _____ _____ _____

6. flat   _____ _____ _____

Activity: Make three new sentences of your own. Use two new words in each sentence.

1. _____

2. _____

3. _____

Answer Key

Lesson 1
1. D   3. A   5. B
2. E   4. C

Activity
1. population: the number of people living in a particular area
2. populous: having or containing a lot of people
3. skyscraper: a very tall building
4. suburbs: an area outside of a city with houses
5. superhuman: beyond normal human abilities

Lesson 2
1. gargantuan
2. brunch
3. waffle
4. cheeseburger
5. pineapple

Activity
Accept reasonable responses.

Lesson 3
1. E   3. A   5. B
2. D   4. C

Activity
1. trophy   4. multicolored
2. triumph   5. metal
3. principal

Lesson 4
1. leadership   4. mettle
2. endanger   5. jittery
3. panic

Activity
1. A   3. S   5. S
2. A   4. A

Lesson 5
1. E   3. C   5. D
2. B   4. A

Activity
Accept reasonable responses.

Lesson 6
1. D   3. A   5. B
2. E   4. C

Activity
1. calm   4. speak
2. dance   5. table
3. darkness

Lesson 7
1. career   4. task
2. wild   5. pain
3. mitt

Activity
1. C   3. A   5. E
2. D   4. B

Lesson 8
1. E   3. A   5. B
2. D   4. C

Activity
1. atlas   4. government
2. capital   5. review
3. exam

Allow appropriate responses for students' sentences.

Lesson 9
1. E   3. D   5. C
2. B   4. A

Activity
1. flexible   4. trainer
2. pretzel   5. graceful
3. ballet

Lesson 10
1. misbehave
2. squirm
3. prank
4. vandal
5. kindergarten

Activity
Answers will vary.

Lesson 11
1. A   3. D   5. B
2. E   4. C

Activity
1. vacant   4. cellar
2. garage   5. mammoth
3. hillside

Lesson 12
1. annual   4. proceeds
2. marina   5. overcast
3. pecan

Activity
1. ocean   4. raincoat
2. berry   5. losses
3. calendar

Lesson 13
1. D   3. A   5. E
2. B   4. C

Activity
1. politician   4. eldest
2. orbit   5. feat
3. voyage

Lesson 14
1. muscles   4. navigate
2. kayak   5. collapse
3. exhausted

Activity
1. D   3. B   5. E
2. A   4. C

Lesson 15
1. E   3. B   5. D
2. A   4. C

Activity
1. helm   4. essential
2. drowsy   5. surroundings
3. conform

Lesson 16
1. infant   4. foal
2. offspring   5. fawn
3. cygnet

Activity
1. infant   4. foal
2. fawn   5. offspring
3. cygnet

Lesson 17
1. furious   4. disturb
2. beehive   5. curious
3. lawn

Activity
1. pleased   4. disturb
2. dog collar   5. uninterested
3. lawn

Lesson 18
1. B   3. A   5. C
2. D   4. E

Activity
1. assign   4. slumber
2. homework   5. uniform
3. rapidly

Accept reasonable responses for students' sentences.

Lesson 19
1. waterfall   4. rowboat
2. scorekeeper   5. sandbox
3. turtleneck

Activity
Answers will vary.

Lesson 20
1. eyesight   4. rustle
2. limbs   5. contentment
3. chirp

Activity
1. eyesight   4. chirp
2. limbs   5. contentment
3. rustle

Lesson 21
1. B   3. D   5. C
2. A   4. E

Activity
1. luxurious
2. tourists
3. paved
4. destination
5. transform

Lesson 22
1. E   3. A   5. D
2. C   4. B

Activity
1. modern
2. erected
3. mysteries
4. monument
5. site

Lesson 23
1. C   3. B   5. E
2. D   4. A

Activity
1. inactivity   4. cooperate
2. repair   5. available
3. displeasure

Lesson 24
1. vocal   4. performer
2. solo   5. Bravo
3. anxious

Activity
1. anxious: uneasy, worried
2. bravo: an expression of approval
3. performer: a person who entertains others
4. solo: an action performed by one person
5. vocal: of the human voice

Lesson 25
1. B   3. E   5. A
2. C   4. D

Activity
1. formula   4. feeble
2. ban   5. gracious
3. assist

Lesson 26
1. unattended   4. natural
2. tidy   5. habitat
3. container

Activity
1. habitat   4. tidy
2. container   5. unattended
3. natural

Lesson 27
1. D   3. C   5. E
2. B   4. A

Activity
1. amazement
2. apparent
3. artificial
4. evacuate
5. infrequently

Accept reasonable responses for students' sentences.

Lesson 28
1. peak   4. descended
2. flurry   5. futile
3. sleigh

Answer Key (cont.)

Activity
1. sunshine
2. futile
3. roller skates
4. valley
5. went up

Lesson 29
1. chores   4. sigh
2. prefer   5. lovable
3. maintain

Activity
1. chores   4. prefer
2. lovable   5. sigh
3. maintain

Accept reasonable responses for students' sentences.

Lesson 30
1. D   3. B   5. A
2. C   4. E

Activity
1. eavesdrop   4. vanish
2. celebrity   5. hobbies
3. artistic

Lesson 31
1. E   3. C   5. D
2. B   4. A

Activity
1. impressed   4. release
2. pollution   5. recycle
3. hybrid

Lesson 32
1. yearn   4. guarantee
2. hoarse   5. startled
3. frightful

Activity
1. frightful   4. startled
2. guarantee   5. yearn
3. hoarse

Accept reasonable responses for students' sentences.

Lesson 33
1. B   3. A   5. C
2. E   4. D

Activity
1. pedestal   4. transplant
2. portable   5. host
3. nonstop

Lesson 34
1. C   3. A   5. E
2. B   4. D

Activity
1. aqueduct
2. blueprint
3. consider
4. mathematical
5. sewer

Accept reasonable responses for students' sentences.

Lesson 35
1. C   3. E   5. B
2. A   4. D

Activity
1. A   3. S   5. S
2. A   4. A

Lesson 36
1. A   3. B   5. D
2. E   4. C

Activity
1. S   3. A   5. A
2. A   4. S

Lesson 37
1. E   3. C   5. A
2. D   4. B

Activity
1. E   3. B   5. D
2. C   4. A

Lesson 38
1. council
2. bungalow
3. counsel
4. ingredients
5. entrée

Activity
1. bungalow
2. counsel
3. ingredients
4. entrée
5. council

Lesson 39
1. E   3. C   5. D
2. B   4. A

Activity
1. contain   4. galley
2. escape   5. freighter
3. wharf

Lesson 40
1. B   3. E   5. D
2. C   4. A

Activity
1. academy: a school for studying a special skill
2. commiserate: to feel sorry for, usually because of feeling the same way
3. fatigue: tiredness
4. liberty: freedom
5. troop: soldier

Lesson 41
1. Marathon   4. historic
2. foul   5. infamous
3. invalid

Activity
1. foul
2. historic
3. marathon
4. invalid
5. infamous

Lesson 42
1. B   3. E   5. D
2. A   4. C

Activity
1. abstain
2. splatter
3. receptacle
4. troop
5. prohibited

Lesson 43
1. telethon
2. tiresome
3. vaudeville
4. chitchat
5. bountiful

Activity
1. telethon
2. tiresome
3. bountiful
4. chitchat
5. vaudeville

Lesson 44
1. B   3. D   5. A
2. C   4. E

Activity
1. headquarters
2. barometer
3. turbulent
4. colony
5. archipelago

Lesson 45
1. modem
2. criticism
3. malfunction
4. cumbersome
5. doodad

Activity
Answer will vary.

Lesson 46
1. E   3. C   5. D
2. A   4. B

Activity
1. salmon   4. invalid
2. flimsy   5. neglect
3. faultless

Lesson 47
1. numeral   4. compile
2. numerator 5. clarity
3. string

Activity
1. clarity: clearness
2. compile: to collect or group together
3. numeral: number
4. numerator: the top part of a fraction
5. string: to put together in a line

Lesson 48
1. A   3. E   5. C
2. B   4. D

Activity
1. monosyllabic
2. chemist
3. weird
4. zany
5. novice

Lesson 49
1. skulk
2. abduct
3. accusation
4. blunder
5. treacherous

Activity
1. abduct: to kidnap
2. accusation: saying someone did something bad
3. blunder: a bad mistake
4. skulk: to creep
5. treacherous: mean and dishonest

Lesson 50
1. B   3. C   5. D
2. A   4. E

Activity
1. D   3. C   5. A
2. E   4. B

Lesson 51
1. moped   4. gym
2. gas   5. deli
3. vet

Activity
1. deli   4. moped
2. gas   5. vet
3. gym

Accept reasonable responses for students' sentences.

Lesson 52
1. B   3. C   5. E
2. D   4. A

Activity
1. D   3. E   5. B
2. A   4. C

Answer Key *(cont.)*

Lesson 53
1. boulder   4. desert
2. geology   5. geography
3. quicksand

Activity
1. quicksand
2. geography, desert
3. geology, boulder

Lesson 54
1. sweltering   4. vessel
2. waterfront   5. driftwood
3. yacht

Activity
Answers will vary.

Lesson 55
1. triangle   4. landmark
2. polygon   5. pentagon
3. octagon

Activity
1. B   3. A   5. C
2. E   4. D

Lesson 56
1. D   3. C   5. A
2. B   4. E

Activity
1. china
2. gobbledygook
3. limerick
4. notion
5. pledge
Accept reasonable responses for students' sentences.

Lesson 57
1. trampoline   4. unicorn
2. unicycle   5. mare
3. saxophone

Activity
1. saxophone   4. unicorn
2. trampoline   5. unicycle
3. mare

Lesson 58
1. B   3. D   5. A
2. C   4. E

Activity
1. C   3. B   5. D
2. A   4. E

Lesson 59
1. patio   4. identical
2. bore   5. dissimilar
3. artist

Activity
1. amateur   4. patio
2. identical   5. same
3. fill

Lesson 60
1. C   3. A   5. B
2. D   4. E

Activity
1. bore
2. funny bone
3. popular
4. preview
5. probability
Accept reasonable responses for students' sentences.

Lesson 61
1. supermarket
2. takeout
3. neighborhood
4. displease
5. appear

Activity
1. supermarket
2. takeout
3. neighborhood
4. displease
5. appear

Lesson 62
1. A   3. B   5. C
2. D   4. E

Activity
1. eerie   4. photocopier
2. enlarge   5. postscript
3. excited
Accept reasonable responses for students' sentences.

Lesson 63
1. kinship   4. ravioli
2. foreign   5. condo
3. futon

Activity
1. blanket
2. ravioli
3. familiar
4. hello
5. disassociation

Lesson 64
1. A   3. B   5. E
2. D   4. C

1. diameter   4. textbook
2. geometry   5. typo
3. congruent

Lesson 65
1. polliwog   4. bass
2. aquarium   5. fret
3. aquatic

Activity
1. aquarium: a glass tank in which fish are kept
2. aquatic: of or having to do with water

3. bass: a common freshwater fish
4. fret: worry
5. polliwog: a tadpole

Lesson 66
1. C   3. A   5. E
2. D   4. B

Activity
1. bass: an instrument usually having four strings that can play lower notes than a guitar
2. flashy: showing off
3. fret: each of a series of bars or ridges on the fingerboard of a stringed instrument
4. jazz: an American type of mostly instrumental music in which the musicians play in response to what each other is doing
5. joyous: extremely happy

Lesson 67
1. heliport
2. depot
3. royalty
4. caboose
5. suite

Activity
1. caboose   4. royalty
2. heliport   5. suite
3. depot

Lesson 68
1. D   3. E   5. A
2. C   4. B

Activity
1. jovial   3. nimble
2. romp   4. doe, buck

Lesson 69
1. ski   4. sunburn
2. laziness   5. envious
3. motel

Activity
1. C   3. E   5. B
2. A   4. D

Lesson 70
1. D   3. E   5. B
2. A   4. C

Activity
1. E   3. A   5. D
2. C   4. B

Lesson 71
1. trickle   4. twirl
2. umbrella   5. torrent
3. unfurl

Activity
1. unfurl   4. twirl
2. torrent   5. trickle
3. umbrella

Lesson 72
1. E   3. D   5. B
2. A   4. C

Activity
1. E   3. B   5. A
2. C   4. D

Lesson 73
1. avocado
2. scoop
3. scoop
4. mayonnaise
5. gingerbread
6. sandwich

Activity
Answers will vary. Be sure the students use the correct form of the word "scoop" in sentences #2 and #3.

Lesson 74
1. C   3. E   5. B
2. D   4. A

Activity
1. bolder: braver, more confident
2. comport: to behave
3. corps: a body of troops with special duties
4. desert: to give up or leave
5. methodical: very careful and exact

Lesson 75
1. C   3. A   5. E
2. F   4. D   6. B

Activity
1. D   3. E   5. C
2. B   4. F   6. A

Lesson 76
1. bandit   4. heroic
2. hullabaloo   5. refuse
3. minute   6. gang

Activity
1. bandit: a type of criminal who steals
2. gang: a small group
3. heroic: like a hero; brave
4. hullabaloo: a lot of noise and activity
5. minute: 60 seconds
6. refuse: to say "no" to something

Lesson 77
1. E   3. D   5. F
2. C   4. B   6. A

Answer Key *(cont.)*

Activity
1. bridal   4. crews
2. coarse   5. course
3. cruise   6. bridle

Lesson 78
1. unique   4. sonar
2. laser   5. radar
3. scuba   6. quasar

Activity
1. C   3. E   5. A
2. F   4. D   6. B

Lesson 79
1. A   3. E   5. C
2. F   4. D   6. B

Activity
1. A   3. D   5. C
2. F   4. B   6. E

Lesson 80
1. rhyme   4. meter
2. haiku   5. couplet
3. sonnet   6. simile

Activity
Answer will vary.

Lesson 81
1. B   3. D   5. A
2. C   4. F   6. E

Activity
1. bikini, ridiculous
2. holiday, glimmer
3. barbecue, allow

Lesson 82
1. C   3. E   5. D
2. F   4. A   6. B

Activity
1. snare   4. car stereo
2. break apart   5. dismiss
3. acting   6. approve

Lesson 83
1. E   3. D   5. C
2. A   4. F   6. B

Activity
1. S   3. A   5. A
2. S   4. S   6. A

Lesson 84
1. underground
2. earthquake
3. volcano
4. dormant
5. cyclone
6. whirlpool

Activity
1. cyclone: a very large circular storm that forms at sea
2. dormant: not active; sleeping

3. earthquake: a shaking of the earth caused by the movement on or beneath the surface
4. underground: beneath the surface of the earth
5. volcano: a mountain or hill through which lava may force its way out of the earth
6. whirlpool: a funnel-shaped, spinning area of water

Lesson 85
1. A   3. F   5. C
2. E   4. B   6. D

Activity
Answer will vary.

Lesson 86
1. oasis   4. vineyard
2. plateau   5. peninsula
3. valley   6. gorge

Activity
1. gorge: a narrow opening between hills, often with a river at the bottom of it
2. oasis: an area in the desert that has water and plant life
3. peninsula: a patch of land that juts out into the water
4. plateau: a high, flat area of land
5. valley: a low-lying stretch of land surrounded by hills or mountains
6. vineyard: an area with vines used for growing grapes for winemaking

Lesson 87
1. C   3. B   5. F
2. E   4. D   6. A

Activity
1. a meat
2. a sauce
3. a storage area
4. a fruit
5. a vegetable
6. a taste

Lesson 88
1. grad   4. ref
2. fan   5. mic
3. limo   6. coed

Activity
1. limo   4. fan
2. grad   5. ref
3. coed   6. mic

Lesson 89
1. B   3. C   5. E
2. A   4. F   6. D

Activity
1. considerate: thoughtful
2. illegal: against the law
3. intersection: a place where two (or more) streets cross each other
4. kilometer: 1,000 meters (0.61 miles)
5. pedal: a control that is pushed by the foot
6. pedestrian: a person who is walking

Lesson 90
1. strait
2. hydroplane
3. isthmus
4. delta
5. hydroelectric
6. tributary

Activity
1. E   3. B   5. F
2. C   4. D   6. A

Lesson 91
1. F   3. A   5. D
2. C   4. E   6. B

Activity
1. unicycle   4. uninterested
2. sycamore   5. ingredient
3. helmet   6. igloo

Lesson 92
1. flabbergasted
2. fiddlesticks
3. magazine
4. oxygen
5. daunting
6. lollygag

Activity
1. telephone   4. radio
2. bored   5. lollygag
3. simple   6. "Boo!"

Lesson 93
1. D   3. B   5. C
2. E   4. F   6. A

Activity
1. tarantula   4. impala
2. school   5. gaggle
3. sardines   6. alligator

Lesson 94
1. C   3. D   5. A
2. E   4. F   6. B

Activity
Answer will vary.

Lesson 95
1. generally
2. rash
3. declaration
4. substantial
5. paratroops
6. permanent

Activity
Answer will vary.

Lesson 96
1. F   3. B   5. D
2. C   4. E   6. A

Activity
1. B   3. A   5. C
2. F   4. E   6. D

Lesson 97
1. sluggish
2. pajamas
3. bewildered
4. frisky
5. compliment
6. blissful

Activity
1. A   3. S   5. A
2. S   4. A   6. S

Lesson 98
1. F   3. B   5. D
2. E   4. A   6. C

Activity
1. A   3. S   5. S
2. A   4. A   6. S

Lesson 99
1. declare   4. dictator
2. biannual   5. veep
3. predict   6. reform

Activity
1. F   3. E   5. A
2. B   4. C   6. D

Lesson 100
1. D   3. F   5. A
2. E   4. B   6. C

Activity
1. interesting
2. dictate
3. masterpiece
4. company
5. illiterate
6. manuscript

Lesson 101
1. recreation   4. flair
2. recreation   5. flat
3. flare   6. flat

Activity
Answer will vary.

Word Index—By Lesson Number

Word Index—By Lesson Number *(cont.)*

fret 66
frightful 32
frisky 97
funny bone 60
furious 17
futile 28
futon 63

G

gaggle 93
galley 39
gang 76
garage 11
gargantuan 2
gas 51
gas 52
gasp 5
generally 95
geography 53
geology 53
geometry 64
gingerbread 73
glimmer 81
gobbledygook 56
gorge 86
government 8
graceful 9
gracious 25
grad 88
guarantee 32
gym 51

H

habitat 26
haiku 80
hairbrush 19
haphazard 35
hazardous 98
headquarters 44
heedless 96
heliport 67
helm 15
heroic 76
hillside 11
historic 41
hoarse 32
hobbies 30
hobnob 50
hodgepodge 91

holiday 81
homework 18
host 33
hullabaloo 76
hybrid 31
hydroelectric 90
hydroplane 90

I

identical 59
illegal 89
illiterate 100
impala 93
impressed 31
infamous 41
infant 16
infrequently 27
ingredients 38
interesting 100
intersection 89
invalid 41
invalid 46
irrational 96
irresponsible 85
isthmus 90

J

jazz 66
jittery 4
journalism 82
jovial 68
joyous 66

K

kayak 14
ketchup 87
kilometer 89
kimono 91
kindergarten 10
kinship 63

L

landmark 55
larder 87
laser 78
lawn 17
laziness 69
lead 37
leadership 4
liberty 40
limbs 20

limerick 56
limo 88
lollygag 92
loot 94
lovable 29
lunchtime 19
lute 94
luxurious 21

M

magazine 92
maintain 29
malformed 46
malfunction 45
mammoth 11
manuscript 100
marathon 41
mare 57
marina 12
masterpiece 100
mathematical 34
mayonnaise 73
mechanic 85
merge 82
metal 3
meter 80
methodical 74
mettle 4
mic 88
minute (adj.) 75
minute (n.) 76
misbehave 10
mitt 7
modem 45
modern 22
monorail 70
monosyllabic 48
monument 22
moped 51
motel 69
multicolored 3
multipurpose 70
muscles 14
mysteries 22

N

natural 26
navigate 14
necessary 36

neighborhood 61
nimble 68
nonstop 33
notion 56
novice 48
numeral 47
numerator 47
numerous 96

O

oasis 86
object (n.) 94
object (v.) 94
octagon 55
offspring 16
okra 87
onomatopoeia 79
optimism 83
orbit 13
ordinary 83
outstanding 83
overcast 12
oxygen 92

P

pain 7
pajamas 97
panic 4
paratroops 95
pathetic 98
patio 59
paved 21
peak 28
pecan 12
pedal 89
pedestal 33
pedestrian 89
peninsula 86
pentagon 55
perfectionist 83
performer 24
permanent 95
personification 79
photocopier 62
photograph 5
pineapple 2
plateau 86
playground 19
pledge 56

Word Index—By Lesson Number *(cont.)*

politician 13
polliwog 65
pollution 31
polygon 55
popular 60
population 1
populous 1
portable 33
postscript. 62
pram 91
prank 10
predict 99
prefer. 29
prehistoric 58
present (n.) 94
present (v.) 94
pretzel 9
preview 60
principal 3
probability. 60
proceeds 12
profitable 72
prohibited 42

Q

quasar 78
quicksand 53
quivering 98

R

radar 78
railroad 19
rapidly. 18
rash 95
ravioli 63
receptacle 42
recreation 101
recycle. 31
ref 88
reform 99
refuse (n.) 75
refuse (v.) 76
release 31
remarkable. 70
repair 23
report 72
review 8
rhyme 80
ridiculous. 81

rodeo 5
romp 68
rowboat 19
royalty 67
rustle 20

S

sandbox 19
sandwich 73
sardines 93
saxophone 57
school 93
scoop 73
scorekeeper 19
scuba 78
sensible 83
sewer 34
shiver. 6
shriek. 6
sigh 29
simile. 80
site 22
sketch 37
ski 69
skulk 49
skull. 58
skyscraper 1
sleigh 28
sluggish 97
slumber 18
smog 52
snafu 83
snare 82
solo 24
sonar 78
sonnet 80
spaceship. 19
speedometer 85
spellbound. 91
splatter. 42
squawk 79
squirm 10
startled. 32
strait. 90
string 47
substantial 95
suburbs 1
succulent 87
suite 67

sunburn 69
superhuman. 1
supermarket. 61
surroundings 15
sweltering 54
sympathy. 46
syrup 75

T

takeout. 61
tangerine 75
tarantula. 93
task 7
taxi. 85
teammate. 36
telethon 43
textbook. 64
thermometer 91
thrash. 5
tidy 26
tiresome. 43
torrent 71
tourists. 21
trainer 9
trampoline 57
transcontinental 72
transform. 21
transplant. 33
transport 72
treacherous 49
triangle 55
tributary. 90
trickle 71
triumph 3
troop 40
troop 42
trophy 3
turbulent 44
turtleneck. 19
tuxedo 85
twirl 71
typo 64

U

umbrella 71
unattended. 26
underground 84
undertaking 23
uneasy 6

unfurl. 71
unicorn 57
unicycle. 57
uniform 18
unique 78
unstable 98

V

vacant 11
vain 52
valid. 96
valley. 86
vandal 10
vanish 30
vaudeville 43
veep. 99
vein 52
vessel. 54
vet 51
vet 52
veto 82
vigor 98
vineyard. 86
vocal 24
volcano 84
voyage. 13

W

waffle 2
waterfall 19
waterfront 54
weird 48
wharf. 39
whirlpool 84
wild 7
windshield. 82

X

Y

yacht 54
yearn 32

Z

zany. 48
zip 79